WARRANTY SERVICE

FOR BUILDERS AND REMODELERS

Carol Smith

Home Builder Press®
National Association of Home Builders
1201 15th Street, NW
Washington, DC 20005-2800
(800) 223-2665

This publication is designed to provide accurate and authoritative information in regard to the subject matter covered. It is sold with the understanding that the publisher is not engaged in rendering legal, accounting, or other professional service. If legal advice or other expert assistance is required, the services of a competent professional person should be sought.

—From a Declaration of Principles jointly adopted by a Committee of the American Bar Association and a Committee of Publishers and Associations.

Warranty Service for Builders and Remodelers
ISBN 0-86718-367-5

Copyright © 1991 by Home Builder Press® of the National Association of Home Builders

Library of Congress Cataloging-in-Publication Data

Smith, Carol, 1946-
    Warranty service for builders and remodelers / Carol Smith.
      p. cm.
    ISBN 0-86718-367-5
    1. Construction industry—Customer services. 2. Warranty.
  I. Title,
  HD9715.A2S547   1991
690'.068'8—dc20   91-28103
                                              CIP

For further information, please contact:
  Home Builder Press®
  National Association of Home Builders
  15th and M Streets, N.W.
  Washington, D.C. 20005
  800/368-5242

12/91 Scott/Cap City 3000
10/96 Reprint McN&G 700

CONTENTS

FIGURES

FOREWORD

Developing a good relationship with customers is hard work.
Anyone searching for easy answers or shortcuts is in for a big
surprise. Creating and maintaining good customer relationships
takes time, effort, imagination, sensitivity, objectivity, and a
sense of fair play. And ethics, integrity, awareness, forethought,
analysis, anticipation, planning . . . and more. The task can be
very complicated, or it can be very simple. It can be annoying,
and it can be a lot of fun. Most of the time, good customer service is all of the above.

Today's builders and remodelers have broadened their view of
what is involved in establishing good customer relations. Delivering the home was once thought to be the end of the builder's
involvement. Builders quickly turned their attention to the next
sale, the next closing. But today, customer service is no longer
thought of as merely attending to warranty obligations. That
attitude has been found to work only in the short term. In the
long term, the "take the money and run" attitude hurts business
not only for the specific builder or remodeler, but for everyone in
the new home construction or remodeling business. Now, customer service is seen as everything that builders or remodelers do
for, to, or with their customers.

Builders and remodelers may sometimes think their product is
new construction; really, it is *homes*. The sale of such a product
does not end when the final payment changes hands. Once the
new house or remodeling work is turned over to customers, the
treatment they receive in the form of follow-up communication
and warranty service adds a vital contribution to the product.
How customers are treated strongly affects the quality of their

experience with the product, and consequently their opinion about the company.

As they have expanded their view of service, builders and remodelers have discovered that warranty service—far from being a "necessary evil"—is a valuable potential marketing tool. With that new appreciation has come a realization that planning and control are needed if warranty service is to be effective and efficient in that role.

Customer satisfaction is an elusive target. But its benefits in the marketplace cannot be ignored. In today's highly competitive residential construction industry, the builders and remodelers who come to terms with this aspect of business will have a real advantage. Customer satisfaction contributes to a healthier bottom line, continued positive growth, and increased professional image.

This book is not just a "how to" for warranty service procedures. It also examines customer expectations about warranty service and how those expectations can (and should) be adjusted. It provides a perspective on where warranty fits into a larger customer relations program. With each home or remodeling job, the builder or remodeler creates not just a home for the customer, but a piece of the company's image as well. In that process, the challenge is to satisfy the home buyer and at the same time keep costs under control.

It sometimes seems this challenge cannot be met, that too many factors are involved, that control and influence are overwhelmed. But if examined one task at a time, warranty service becomes manageable, measurable, controllable. With this in mind, *Warranty Service for Builders and Remodelers* examines the challenge task by task and considers possible approaches.

Much of what is written in this book could apply to any business, but its specific focus is the home building and remodeling industries. These industries offer particular challenges. In the final analysis, the individual builder or remodeler will be the best judge of the philosophies, methods, and techniques the book discusses. Within legal boundaries, there are many right answers to warranty issues, many methods that can work. These solutions will be slightly different for each organization. There is, of course, a wrong answer as well: to do nothing and let chance control this important aspect of business.

The objective of *Warranty Service* is to assist builders and remodelers in arriving at a constructive way of thinking about warranty. Once provided with the tools for analyzing the questions, builders and remodelers will quickly adapt them to achieve their goal of a warranty program that serves both their customers and their companies.

Because remodelers are certainly builders even though not all builders are remodelers, in this book the term builder generally has been used to designate both builders and remodelers. Where specific points apply to one or the other only, or require some adjustment, attention is drawn to this fact. Additionally, the terms warranty manager and warranty department refer not only to any specific employee or group that might hold these titles in a larger firm, but also to the frequent situation where one person wears many hats, including both of these.

Several publications and organizations mentioned in this book offer more detailed information about various aspects of warranty service. Builders and remodelers may wish to contact some of the following groups:

The Home Builders Institute, Home Builder Press, and the National Research Center are all at the National Association of Home Builders, 15th and M Streets, NW, Washington, DC 20005, telephone (800) 368-5242. The Home Builders Institute offers a wide variety of training materials and programs; the pamphlet "Your New Home and How to Take Care of It" is published by Home Builder Press; and the *Home Builder's Guide to Fire-Retardant Plywood: Evaluation, Testing, and Replacement* is available with two legal attachments, "Legal Aspects of the Fire-Retardant Plywood Situation," and "Fire Retardant Plywood and Customer Relations," from the National Research Center, telephone (301) 249-4000.

The Magnuson-Moss Act is reprinted in full in the NAHB publication, *New Home Warranties and the Magnuson-Moss Act: A Primer for Builders*, second edition. This publication is available through the Public Affairs Department at NAHB. A copy of the law also may be obtained by contacting the Federal Trade Commission, Public Reference Branch, Washington, DC, 20580.

To obtain a copy of "A Business Person's Guide to Federal Warranty Law," contact the Superintendent of Documents, U.S. Government Printing Office, Washington, DC 20402, telephone (202) 783-3238.

ABOUT THE AUTHOR

Carol Smith is a leading customer relations consultant in the home building industry. She lives in Littleton, Colorado, where she writes and publishes *Home Address*, a monthly newsletter that focuses on customer service information for building professionals.

Ms. Smith has extensive experience in all aspects of the building industry. During her 16 years in the building business, she has held such positions as walk-through representative (over 700 walk-throughs), construction superintendent, real estate broker, property manager, and mortgage officer. She is a frequent speaker at state and local home builders association functions, and she is a featured speaker at the annual convention of the National Association of Home Builders. For Home Builder Press, Ms. Smith co-authored the second edition of *Customer Service for Home Builders* with William Young, and authored *The Positive Walk-Through: Your Blueprint for Success*.

ACKNOWLEDGMENTS

The author would like to acknowledge the contributions of Robert L. Mitchell, President, and Frank Connoley, Vice President of Construction, Architecture and Purchasing for Mitchell and Best, Rockville, MD; also Mary DiCrescenzo, Associate Litigation Counsel, Litigation and Legal Services Department, and William Young, Director of Consumer Affairs/Public Liaison at the National Association of Home Builders, who reviewed and commented on the manuscript. This book was produced under the general direction of Kent Colton, NAHB Executive Vice President, in association with NAHB staff members James E. Johnson, Jr., Staff Vice President, Operations and Information Services; Adrienne Ash, Assistant Staff Vice President, Publishing Services; Rosanne O'Connor, Director of Publications; Sharon Costello, Assistant Director of Publications; and David Rhodes, Art Director.

WARRANTY AS A PART OF SERVICE

Who Needs Warranties?

As any customer will quickly point out, the best service is not needing service. Certainly, if nothing ever broke, no one would need warranties. But builders create a product that combines natural and man-made materials. These materials are assembled by human beings who possess varying levels of experience and ability, moods and attitudes. Under these circumstances, errors and imperfections are a fact of life; therefore, builders must be prepared to back up their products with effective action when problems occur.

Wise builders use their warranty experiences to improve their product, minimizing the expense and nuisance of future call-backs from customers. The goal is to put the warranty department out of work. Although builders may never completely accomplish this objective, working toward it can bring the twin advantages of higher product quality and lower repair costs. Ultimately, this effort benefits the customer, the builder, and the industry.

Most builders and remodelers recognize their legal obligations to warrant their products. Some perceive this obligation as just a necessary evil; others find that using warranties contributes to a positive reputation and future business growth. The challenge is to organize warranty service to

- satisfy the customer,
- ensure that costs are reasonable,
- minimize conflicts and confusion, and
- maximize the potential for referrals and repeat business.

Because so many variables are involved, builders with the best of intentions sometimes fail to meet their own service objectives. The task becomes easier, however, when builders or remodelers focus precisely on clear goals, then identify and develop the tools they need to reach them.

Warranty's Role in a Service Program

Until recently, many builders equated customer service with warranty repairs. With the growth in understanding of what a comprehensive customer service program includes, complaint-department thinking has been replaced by a recognition that warranty and customer service are *not* the same thing. Warranty is one part—a vitally important part—of customer service; but it is not all that makes up service or the builder's service image.

Today, customer service is understood to include everything that happens between a customer and a company. Every interaction between the customer and anyone associated with a builder contributes to that customer's impression of the organization, and ultimately to the builder's overall reputation. Every interaction has the potential to affect what the customer will think, feel, and say about the firm, and can therefore affect future business. For builders, customer service begins with the first telephone call or the first visit and continues *throughout* the relationship with the customer, including the warranty period.

Phases of the Customer Relationship

To acquire a good overall service image, a builder must coordinate and control all phases of the customer relationship. The following four steps can help builders manage this process.

Communication. Honest and forthright communication begins at the point of sale. For a home builder, this includes having models that accurately show the product, clearly defining options, and providing complete information about the orientation or walk-through and warranty service. For remodelers, it includes providing a precise and thorough description of the materials and methods to be used, together with an accurate drawing and carefully outlined terms of payment, warranty coverage, and other conditions. The sales agreement should specify what type of warranty the customer will receive from the builder. The objective is to eliminate surprises and discuss all aspects of the work to be done while the customer's expectations are still flexible.

> **Four Steps to a Positive Customer Relationship**
> 1. Begin with honest and forthright communication at the point of sale.
> 2. Deliver a carefully designed and well-constructed product.
> 3. Provide a relevant, informative walk-through.
> 4. Follow through with effective warranty attention.

Quality. Builders benefit when they deliver a carefully designed and well-constructed product. Increasingly, builders and remodelers are applying quality control techniques to their work. The wisdom of doing the job right the first time is inescapable. By thoroughly communicating standards to employees and subcontractors, then frequently checking work in progress to confirm compliance with those standards, builders can reduce the number of time- and money-consuming repairs. High quality also increases the customer's enjoyment of the product—which can translate to future referrals for the builder.

The Walk-through. A relevant and informative walk-through for a new home usually takes from one and a half to two hours. Although remodelers usually spend less time, investing a few minutes to educate clients and confirm their satisfaction with the work builds customer confidence and adds a professional tone to the final delivery of the product. Even something as simple as installing a new bay window can necessitate an explanation of how the locks operate, how screens come out for cleaning, and what characteristics make the window energy efficient. Immediate, effective attention to any defects noted during the walk-through creates a high level of customer confidence that will carry over into the warranty period.

Warranty. Effective warranty attention is essential. When a problem arises, the customer expects it to be corrected. While this sounds simple on the surface, because of the wide variety of things that can go wrong, responding well is not so simple. Nonetheless, the builder with a smoothly functioning system for correcting mistakes can resolve problems efficiently and keep the customer's good will.

From this perspective, it is easy to see that a positive service image is the product of doing many things well. A great many customer interactions have already taken place before the product is considered to be *in warranty*. The company's warranty manager, warranty staff, or—in smaller organizations—the person assigned to handle warranties, inherits the home, the customer, and the customer's opinions. It is neither fair nor realistic to delegate all responsibility for the company's service image to the warranty department; that image has already been established long before the customer reports the first warranty item.

Consider the processes involved in driving an automobile: The vehicle's design alone is insufficient to ensure safe travel. A driver must be able to turn, stop, accelerate, navigate, prevent or fix mechanical breakdowns, all the while watching out for the mistakes of other drivers. All this and more is needed for the driver to reach a destination safely. The activities involved are very interrelated; a weakness in one area can cause serious problems in another.

Similarly, to arrive successfully at the desired destination in customer service work, each part of the firm must recognize that it affects, and is affected by, the other parts. Many activities must be planned and executed well. Even though professional salespeople may have made a solid presentation that set the customer's expectations appropriately, if the construction crews fail to deliver the promised quality or to finish the job on time, the customer has good reason to be upset.

The fastest, most efficient warranty service will fail to please customers if the sales staff has overpromised the product or services, or if construction was so poorly supervised that the customer must constantly call upon that warranty service. To be successful in the long term, the builder must plan each phase of construction so that customers conclude again and again that they made the right purchasing decision.

The Final Impression

Understanding that warranty service is one part of an overall service program in no way lessens its importance. A builder's relationship with a customer lasts not for hours, days, or even weeks, but for years. The longest segment of this relationship, the builder's warranty service also is remembered by homeowners simply because it comes last.

The treatment a customer receives during warranty offers the builder a final opportunity to overcome any previous problems and regain the customer's respect. Conversely, sloppy or inadequate warranty service can destroy the results of all the earlier good work. The customer's opinion evolves through each stage of the home-buying or remodeling process. The resulting customer attitude can support or haunt the builder for years.

A Complex Challenge

Implementing and maintaining an effective warranty service program is further complicated by the builder's efforts to balance specific legal obligations, an inevitably tight budget, and the customer's expectations. Even the most clear-cut situations require timely and courteous responses, involving accurate communication of many details. Day-to-day warranty work often is made up of unique situations, gray areas, fuzzy boundaries, personal opinions and instincts, paradoxes, contradictions, exceptions, judgment calls, and even an occasional honest mistake. To handle warranty successfully can be difficult, but builders are progressing steadily toward making the task easier and making warranty service an activity that supports their marketing efforts.

Service Trends Affecting Warranty

From effective sales and service training to more efficient computers and other technological developments, several trends are helping to shape warranty service in the 1990s. This chapter closes with a look at eleven trends builders have encountered.

Increased Sophistication

It is frequently said that today's consumer is more sophisticated than ever. While that is certainly true, it is equally true that builders also have become more sophisticated. Differentiation in the marketplace through effective service now is recognized as a valuable strategy for increasing sales. Businesspeople generally have a better understanding of what creates a satisfied customer and a profound respect for word-of-mouth advertising. Builders today are applying these insights and taking control of service.

Blank Checks Not Required

In the past, many businesspeople believed that to increase customer satisfaction they had to increase spending, to say "yes" to any customer demand. While it may be practical for some businesses, this "blank check" approach does not work for builders. Fortunately, there is an effective and acceptable alternative: educating the customer and adjusting his or her expectations.

One of the keys to achieving customer satisfaction is informing the customer early about what services come with the product. An informed customer who accepts these terms and then commits to the purchase is more likely to remain satisfied.

Sales Staff Involvement

To successfully adjust a customer's expectations, the process must begin early, with the sales staff. But before the sales professionals can educate customers, they must themselves know and understand the necessary information. Sharing ideas and points of view among sales, construction, and warranty personnel can smooth out many rough spots in builder programs. An involved, informed sales team makes promises at the point of sale that the builder can meet—or even exceed. When this is done, the satisfaction of the customer becomes not only attainable, but probable.

Better Product Through Quality Control

Increased commitment to quality control helps keep costs down and keep customers satisfied. Builders have come to understand that ultimately it is cheaper and faster to do the job right the first time. Keeping the promises that the salesperson made to the customer is much easier if the builder can consistently produce the product intended. A better product requires fewer adjustments later and makes a better impression on the customer. In a sense, the warranty coverage builders provide to customers is the last step in the builder's quality control efforts. It serves the builder as a valuable source of feedback about the product and the communications that have occurred with the customer. In some cases, builders discover that future problems can be avoided by changing the sales presentation or the written documents in order to communicate with the customer more clearly.

More Structure and Planning

To achieve better control of their customer service, builders are planning service programs as carefully as they plan their products. Many builders have devoted much time and effort to identifying customers' needs and developing procedures and systems that serve those needs. What builders previously left to chance they now methodically analyze and organize. Facts are replacing assumptions. Habits and traditions are weighed against information from customer surveys and buyer focus groups. No longer content to allow their business futures to rest on hoped-for goodwill, more and more builders are taking steps to ensure that their customers feel good about their new home purchase or remodeling work.

Longer Warranties

When today's consumers spend their hard-earned income, they naturally expect lasting value in return. Longer warranties and extended service agreements are increasingly common in many industries, including residential construction and remodeling. With more confidence in the overall quality of warranties, builders today are more comfortable providing extended coverage. Not only are the insured warranty programs making structural warranty extensions available (usually in five-year increments), but some builders have increased the materials and workmanship portion of their coverage to two years. In the future, even longer warranties may become the norm.

Courtesy

In our fast-paced world, the few extra moments it takes to be polite are often lost. But personal courtesy is a valuable commodity to customers and a style of service that includes courtesy is very much appreciated. This is one of the elements that can turn "ho-hum" service into excellent service. Seemingly little touches—making an extra follow-up telephone call, providing a thoughtful piece of information, or taking the time to explain a situation instead of simply reacting to it—demonstrate this more caring service attitude.

The emotional tone of any customer transaction contributes to the builder's service image. Today, providing repairs in a grudging manner is unacceptable. Professional habits about setting and keeping appointments, cleaning up after work is completed, and maintaining good follow-up communication make the hands-on part of warranty work more effective and pleasant for all parties concerned.

Selection and Training for Service

Excessive turnover among employees or subcontractors diminishes the benefits of the builder's training investments and can leave the builder starting over again and again. To reduce turnover, builders are screening employees and subcontractors more carefully and conducting more detailed orientations for new additions to the team.

Communicating the builder's service philosophy to all employees and subcontractors—and especially to front line people—contributes to a successful service approach. It serves no one if the builder has a terrific attitude about customers and great ideas about how to care for them but keeps it all a secret. Whether the builder employs two people or two hundred, each one needs to understand the company's service approach and be able to assist the customer in a variety of circumstances.

Cross training of personnel is also increasingly popular. Cross training results in smoother overall operation of the business and greater flexibility when market conditions change. The builder cannot always predict or control who the customer will contact with a question or a problem. By providing all employees with a general knowledge of the various functions in the business, the builder ensures that the customer receives more consistent responses. Customers whose questions are answered promptly, correctly, and consistently are unlikely to feel they are getting "the run around."

Many excellent seminars are available for formal training on customer service. The Home Builders Institute and many local HBA/BIA chapters offer programs specifically developed to address the issues and concerns of builders and remodelers.

Technology

Computers. Predictably, the computer software industry has discovered warranty service. Issuing work orders and organizing mailings are obviously tasks well suited to the computer. But the more dramatic value of computer support for warranty is in the tracking of details: the sorting, categorizing, summarizing, and reporting so useful in warranty work are ideal assignments for a computer. Delegating such detailed paperwork to the computer frees people to communicate with customers. Especially for high-volume transactions, computers can be better than people at identifying repeating problems. For example, where two or three different people are involved in manually issuing, responding to, and filing service orders, recurring patterns easily can go unnoticed.

Videotapes. Videotaping is another technology lending support to service efforts. Builders use taped programs as a training tool at staff meetings, to bring new employees up to date, or as gifts to buyers, informing them about service and maintenance on their homes. A few builders have used videotapes to record construction progress at specific sites, or even to record the walk-through, thereby eliminating questions that might arise later about the condition of the home at delivery. Videotapes given to customers are likely to be shown to family and friends—whereupon they become an advertising tool as well as a service tool. Remodelers can use before-and-after photographs or videotapes in a similar way to provide a visual record of the quality of completed work.

Telecommunications. Communication support is available in a wide variety of styles and prices. Service personnel use digital or voice pagers, two-way radios, or car phones. Voice mail provides backup for busy receptionists and for small offices where staffs must sometimes be away from the telephone. Voice mail is reliable and economical enough for use by companies with limited budgets. Telephone answering machines provide an additional option, as long as customers do not perceive that such devices are being used to avoid or screen their calls. During weekends or holidays and after hours, builders can still make themselves available through telecommunications.

For larger firms telephone "800" service also can assist sales and warranty. Fax machines expedite notification of subs about needed work, especially in emergencies. Increasingly, builders insist that critical subs—HVAC personnel, plumbers, and electricians—provide some means for seven-day, 24-hour emergency communication.

Industry Networking

Communication among builders interested in improving service has increased. Local HBA/BIA chapters and Remodelors™ Councils have set up customer service study groups and committees. Builders observe each other's service practices as closely as design trends. They communicate more openly and share suggestions about what works and what does not. With the recognition that good service improves the overall image of the industry, the old, proprietary attitude toward good solutions is disappearing. As a result, improvement in service is gaining momentum. Builders facing a new situation can call another builder across town or bring the subject up at the next service group meeting. Although it is not always practical to replicate someone else's solution, this exchange of ideas fosters the attitude that solutions *can* be found and stimulates creativity and cooperation.

It is interesting and reassuring to note that industry veterans are arriving at the same fundamental conclusions: Satisfying the customer begins with adjusting expectations, delivering on the promises made in the sales process, providing effective, courteous follow-up service, and listening to customer feedback. Once these basics are firmly in place, the builder can take advantage of the opportunity to add those special touches that make a company unique.

Creative Strategies

One thing all businesspeople can count on is that whatever conditions they are operating under today will soon change. Identifying and responding to a healthy, active market demand is a builder's ongoing challenge. The builder who tries to be all things to all customers may end up being nothing to everyone. A close examination of market niches and analysis of what those specific customers want is essential.

Many factors must be taken into account when developing a product for a particular market niche. But a valuable common denominator for all products is a builder's reputation for integrity. Beyond that, builders who listen carefully to what customers tell them can create unique, effective service programs. The possibilities are limited only by the imagination. To identify programs or features that appeal to target markets, a builder closely considers the character of the customers.

Whether a builder creates a unique approach to warranty or simply focuses on doing a superb job with the basics, concentrated effort will turn warranty into a significant part of the builder's marketing effort. Besides gaining repeat and referral sales, builders and their employees will benefit from increased personal satisfaction and pride.

Armed with a sophisticated understanding of exceptional service and with the proper tools and techniques, it remains for builders to put these advantages to work. This is, admittedly, a challenge, but one that is definitely worth meeting.

WARRANTY TYPES AND LEGAL IMPLICATIONS

Many consumers think of the warranty as a document in fine print that expires three days before the covered item breaks. Dictionaries define warranty in terms of a guarantee. Builders and remodelers know that their warranty represents a commitment to respond when a part of a home fails to perform as intended.

Builders can encounter serious legal and public relations problems if they or their customers misunderstand warranty. Acquiring a basic knowledge of the various types of warranties, staying apprised of legal developments regarding warranties, and making a sincere commitment to fulfill their warranty obligations will help builders prevent damage to their companies' financial stability and reputation. The advice of an attorney familiar with the specific—and constantly changing—state laws regarding warranty is indispensable. The information in this chapter is necessarily general and is intended to provide only a broad perspective.

Implied Warranties

The theory behind the implied warranty obligation is that a buyer is entitled to believe no builder would knowingly sell a defective product. Almost all states recognize implied warranties. Builders who operate in those states are automatically assumed to make certain warranties to their customers. These assumptions can include such concepts as the home being "fit for the intended use" or that it will be "habitable." In states where implied warranties are observed, this assumption carries whether or not a written warranty is provided by the builder. Implied warranties may be upheld in addition to or in spite of what is agreed to in a builder's written warranty. If implied warranty laws conflict with the builder's warranty, the implied warranty is likely to be enforced by a court. Such a decision by a court effectively nullifies that portion of the builder's warranty that is contrary to implied warranty law.

Implied warranties are based not only on statutes, but also on case law, or precedent; thus, they constantly change as new decisions are issued. It is important that builders remain aware of these laws and recognize the potential liability they may impose.

Implied warranties are unaffected by verbal agreements that the builder and purchaser may enter into in the course of the sale. Courts also may overrule an implied warranty disclaimer that a builder has included in a written warranty agreement. A disclaimer regarding implied warranty states that the builder and the purchaser have agreed that implied warranties will not apply (see Figure 2-1). Generally, courts are moving away from allowing this type of disclaimer. Where they are permitted, however, they must be written clearly and conspicuously (set in large print, using bold type, and all in capitals). Any such disclaimer should be written by an attorney familiar with applicable state laws. Even then, the builder should recognize that the disclaimer cannot provide unfailing protection.

Courts in recent years have upheld the principle of implied warranty and even expanded coverage under implied warranties. Further, depending on the state, protection under the implied warranty concept may apply to both the original and subsequent purchasers. Builders should check with their legal counsel to find out what kinds of coverage they may be liable for under implied warranty statutes or rulings. Builders should be aware of statutes of limitations for claims regarding faulty construction, what defects are covered, and whether or not implied warranty protection extends to subsequent owners of the home.

Express Warranties

An express warranty is a stated warranty. It is a promise made by the builder, either in conversation or in writing, to the buyer. Considering the complexity of their product, builders usually find that a written warranty best serves the needs of their buyers and themselves (see Figure 2-1). A well-written warranty, supported by clear standards, can reduce confusion, prevent disagreements and misinterpretations, and reduce the likelihood that the buyer will claim to have been misled.

Figure 2-1: Sample Builder Warranty
(Assignable, Structural Elements Omitted.)

One-year Limited Warranty Agreement

_____, hereafter called the "Company," extends the following one-year limited warranty to _____, hereafter referred to as "Owner," who has contracted with the Company for purchase of the home located at _____ in _____ County, state of _____, for the purchase price of $_____ (_____).

The commencement date of the warranty is _____, 19_____, and shall extend for a period of ONE YEAR.

1. COVERAGE ON HOME EXCEPT CONSUMER PRODUCTS: The Company expressly warrants to the original Owner and to subsequent Owner of the home that the home will be free from defects in materials and workmanship due to noncompliance with the standards set forth in the One-year Limited Warranty Performance Standards of Material and Workmanship in effect on the date of this warranty, entitled Exhibit A, and which are part of this warranty.

2. COVERAGE ON CONSUMER PRODUCTS: For purposes of this Limited Warranty Agreement, the term "consumer products" means all appliances, equipment and other items which are consumer products for the purposes of the Magnuson-Moss Warranty Act (15 USC, sections 2301-2312) and which are located in the home on the commencement date of the warranty. The Company expressly warrants that all consumer products will, for a period of one-year after the commencement date of this warranty, be free from defects due to noncompliance with generally accepted standards in the state in which the home is located, which assure quality of materials and workmanship. ANY IMPLIED WARRANTIES FOR ANY SUCH CONSUMER PRODUCTS SHALL TERMINATE ON THE SAME DATE AS THE EXPRESS WARRANTY STATED ABOVE. Some states do not allow limitations on how long an implied warranty lasts, so this limitation may not apply to you. The Company hereby assigns to Owner all rights under manufacturers' warranties covering consumer products. Defects in items covered by manufacturers' warranties are excluded from coverage of this limited warranty, and Owner should follow the procedures in the manufacturers' warranties if defects appear in these items. This warranty gives you specific legal rights, and you may have other rights which vary from state to state.

3. COMPANY'S OBLIGATIONS: If a covered defect occurs during the one-year warranty period, the Company agrees to repair, replace, or pay Owner the reasonable cost of repairing or replacing the defective item. The Company's total liability under this warranty is limited to the purchase price of the home stated above. The choice among repair, replacement, or payment is the Company's. Any steps taken by the Company to correct defects shall not act to extend the term of this warranty. All repairs by the Company shall be at no charge to the Owner and shall be performed within a reasonable length of time.

4. OWNER'S OBLIGATION: Owner must provide normal maintenance and proper care of the home according to this warranty, the warranties of manufacturers of consumer products, and generally accepted standards of the state in which the home is located. The Company must be notified in writing, by the original Owner of the existence of any defect before the Company is responsible for the correction of that defect. Written notice of a defect must be received by the Company prior to the expiration of the warranty on that defect and no action at law or in equity may be brought by Owner against the Company for failure to remedy or repair any defect about which the Company has not received timely notice in writing. Owner must provide access to the Company during normal business hours to inspect the defect reported and, if necessary, to take corrective action.

(continued on next page)

(continued from previous page)

5. INSURANCE: In the event the Company repairs or replaces or pays the cost of repairing or replacing any defect covered by this warranty for which the Owner is covered by insurance or a warranty provided by another party, Owner must, upon request of the Company, assign the proceeds of such insurance or other warranty to the Company to the extent of the cost to the Company of such repair or replacement.

6. CONSEQUENTIAL OR INCIDENTAL DAMAGES EXCLUDED: CONSEQUENTIAL OR INCIDENTAL DAMAGES ARE NOT COVERED BY THIS WARRANTY. Some states do not allow the exclusion or limitation of incidental or consequential damages, so the above limitation or exclusion may not apply to you.

7. OTHER EXCLUSIONS: THE FOLLOWING ADDITIONAL ITEMS ARE NOT COVERED BY THIS LIMITED WARRANTY:

  a. Defects in any item which was not part of the original home as constructed by the Company.

  b. Any defect caused by or worsened by negligence, improper maintenance, lack of maintenance, improper action or inaction, willful or malicious acts by any party other than the Company, its employees, agents, or subcontractors.

  c. Normal wear and tear of the home or consumer products in the home.

  d. Loss or damage caused by acts of God, including but not limited to fire, explosion, smoke, water escape, changes which are not reasonably foreseeable in the level of underground water table, glass breakage, windstorm, hail, lightning, falling trees, aircraft, vehicles, flood, and earthquakes.

  e. Any defect or damage caused by changes in the grading or drainage patterns or by excessive watering of the ground of the Owner's property or adjacent property by any party other than the Company, its employees, agents, or subcontractors.

  f. Any defect which does not cause actual loss or damage.

  g. Any loss or damage which arises while the home is being used primarily for nonresidential purposes.

  h. Any damage to the extent it is caused or made worse by the failure of anyone other than the Company or its employees, agents, or subcontractors to comply with the requirements of this warranty or the requirements of warranties of manufacturers of appliances, equipment, or fixtures.

  i. Any defect or damage which is covered by a manufacturer's warranty that has been assigned to Owner under paragraph 2 of this Limited Warranty.

  j. Failure of Owner to take timely action to minimize loss or damage and/or failure of Owner to give the Company timely notice of the defect.

  k. Bodily injury, damage to personal property or damage to real property which is not part of the home which was included in the purchase price stated above.

  l. Insect or animal damage.

(continued on next page)

(continued from previous page)

8. ARBITRATION OF DISPUTE: The Owner shall promptly contact the Company's warranty department regarding any disputes involving this Agreement. If discussions between the parties do not resolve such dispute, then either party may, upon written notice to the other party, submit such dispute to arbitration with each party hereto selecting one arbitrator, who shall then select the third arbitrator. The arbitrators shall proceed under the construction industry rules of the American Arbitration Association. The award of the majority of the arbitrators shall be final, conclusive, and binding upon the parties hereto. The expenses of the arbitrators shall be shared equally, but each party shall bear its own fees and costs.

9. EXCLUSIVE WARRANTY: The Company and Owner agree that this limited warranty on the home is in lieu of all warranties of habitability or workmanlike construction or any other warranties, express or implied, to which Owner might be entitled, except as to consumer products. No employee, subcontractor, or agent of the Company has the authority to change the terms of this One-year Limited Warranty.

DATED the _____ day of _____, 19____.

_____   _____
(Owner)   (Builder)
_____   By_____
(Owner)

Warranty laws vary from state to state. As they would with any legal document, builders and remodelers should consult with a local attorney who is well versed in construction warranties for specific details and conditions that may apply in a particular state and that influence the content and language of a warranty used in that state.

The basic intent of the warranty is to guarantee a certain level of performance for a specified period of time. The document that spells out the terms and conditions can vary somewhat from state to state and from builder to builder. However, specific points must be covered, some involving decisions on the part of the builder. One of the first decisions is whether the warranty should be *full* or *limited*.

Full Warranties

Builders almost never provide full warranties. To be considered a full warranty, coverage must (1) provide remedies for specified defects within a reasonable time and at no charge; (2) contain no limitation on or waiver of implied warranties; (3) provide the purchaser the option of returning the product for a refund if a defect cannot be repaired after a reasonable number of attempts; and (4) apply to subsequent owners.

A full warranty must be designated as such in the title, with the time period mentioned as well. For example, the title could read "Full One-year Warranty" or "Full Two-year Warranty." Because most builder warranties do not provide the option of returning the product for a refund, providing a full warranty is almost unheard-of among builders.

Limited Warranties

Any warranty that does not meet all four criteria for a full warranty is automatically a limited warranty. The term is perfectly descriptive: coverage provided by limited warranties is restricted in some way. Again, the time frame and the word "limited" must appear conspicuously in the title, as in "Limited One-year Warranty," or "Limited Six-month Warranty." The limitations must be clearly described in the text of the document. Again, it must be remembered that providing a limited warranty—however carefully written—does not guarantee the builder release of liability under implied warranty laws.

In express warranties that cover consumer products, federal requirements can govern the exact wording, format, and type sizes used in disclosing information about covered items. These requirements are the result of the Magnuson-Moss Warranty— Federal Trade Commission Improvement Act, Public Law number 93-637, which was signed into law in 1975. In addition to the disclosure requirements of Magnuson-Moss, builders may be required to comply with state laws pertaining to disclosure.

Builder-Backed Warranties

Builder-backed warranties almost always are *express* (written) and *limited* (not full). The common term of coverage is one year for materials and workmanship. Some builder-backed warranties include second-year coverage on mechanical systems. (This coverage parallels that of insured warranties, which are discussed near the end of this chapter.) Some builder-backed warranties also cover structural elements (see Figure 2-2), typically for ten years.

Within the limits of applicable codes and industry standards, the builder using this kind of warranty exercises greater control over what is covered and the standards to be met. In practice, reputable builders are fairly consistent in the standards they follow.

The risks for the builder include the expense of major repairs; in particular, structural damages (such as those resulting from expansive soils) can be very costly to fix. Disputes with customers can be time consuming and expensive as well, with the builder sometimes bearing the costs of implied warranty judgments.

Figure 2-2: Sample Statement of Coverage, Major Structural Defects

For a period of ten years from the commencement date of the warranty, Builder expressly warrants to Owner, and any subsequent Owner of the home, that the home will be free from major structural defects. A major structural defect is defined as being an actual defect in a load-bearing portion of the house which seriously impairs its load-bearing function to the extent that the house is unsafe, unsanitary, or unlivable. For purposes of this definition, the following items comprise the structure of the house:

(a) the foundation system,
(b) load-bearing stud walls,
(c) floor joists,
(d) beams, columns, trusses, and rafters.

This sample is provided for purposes of illustration only. When developing or revising warranty documents or other legal documents, always have them reviewed by an attorney qualified for the state(s) in which they will be used.

For the home buyer with a builder-backed warranty, a major risk is that if the builder goes out of business for some reason, the customer has little recourse. The total warranty relationship is between the customer and the builder, subject to action through dispute settlement procedures or the courts.

In addition to disclosures as required by the Magnuson-Moss Act, builder-backed warranties typically include some additional pieces of information. Figure 2-1 shows a sample limited warranty that includes the following sections.

Builder or Company Name. Appearing in the opening paragraph, this should be the full legal name under which the builder operates the business. The address of the builder's main office often follows; this is the address to which the customer will send any written reports of warranty claims.

Description of Property or Improvement. Also in the opening paragraph, this information identifies the home or work that is referred to by the warranty. The notation usually includes the street address, county, and sometimes the lot, block number, and subdivision. The builder's job number may also be listed.

Consumer Product Warranties Assigned. Coverage on consumer products needs to be assigned, or *passed through* to the home buyer (see Figure 2-3). In this clause, reference often is made to

---

Figure 2-3: Sample Statements Pertaining to Assignability

Notice the difference in wording between paragraph 1 in this example and paragraph 1 in Figure 2-1. Also note the addition of another paragraph covering ASSIGNABILITY. (If using this clause in the warranty shown in Figure 2-1, OTHER EXCLUSIONS would become paragraph 8, and so forth.)

1. COVERAGE ON HOME EXCEPT CONSUMER PRODUCTS: the Company expressly warrants to the original Owner and only to the original Owner of the home that the home will be free from defects in materials and workmanship due to noncompliance with the standards set forth in the Limited Warranty Standards of Material and Workmanship in effect on the date of this warranty, attached hereto as Exhibit A, and which are part of this warranty.

* * *

7. ASSIGNABILITY: The warranty coverages in this Limited Warranty Agreement are provided to the original Owner and may not be assigned to any subsequent owner of the home.

This sample is provided for purposes of illustration only. When developing or revising warranty documents or other legal documents, always have them reviewed by an attorney qualified for the state(s) in which they will be used.

---

the Magnuson-Moss Act. The specific details of the warranties on each of the consumer products are contained in the literature provided by the manufacturers and need not be repeated in the builder's document as long as they are made available to the customer on request.

Insurance. A builder may occasionally repair something for which the purchaser has homeowner insurance coverage. This section provides that, under those circumstances and upon request, proceeds from the insurance will be assigned to the builder up to the amount of expense incurred for the repair.

Dispute Resolution. Although neither the builder nor the customer wants to expect a dispute, disagreements sometimes occur and it is wise to plan for them in advance. Disagreements often can be settled relatively quickly and inexpensively for both sides through mediation, arbitration, or some other preplanned dispute resolution procedure (see chapter 8). Such procedures can be unpleasant, tedious, and time consuming—and they certainly are not free—but they still are generally found to be less burdensome to both parties than going to court.

A customer is unlikely to agree to an alternative dispute resolution procedure once a serious problem has arisen. Therefore, it is advisable for builders to include provisions for such procedures up front in the contract. Whether arbitration or mediation procedures produce binding results is a matter of individual state law. This is another subject that builders should discuss with a local attorney familiar with specific state laws.

Signatures and Date. The date the warranty is signed must appear on the final document. The signatures of the purchasers must appear exactly as the names are presented at the beginning of the warranty. In other words, if "John J. Smith" and "Mary R. Smith" appear at the beginning of the document, both home buyers must include their middle initials in their signatures: "John and Mary Smith" or "John Smith" and "Mary Smith" will not suffice. Very often, the company owner signs as the individual authorized to represent the builder. The homeowners and the builder each receive a copy of the signed warranty. The builder should retain this document in a permanent contract and closing file for the home.

The Magnuson-Moss Act

The Magnuson-Moss Act primarily covers disclosures regarding warranties on consumer products. The Magnuson-Moss Act is directed toward anyone who sells consumer products, not only builders. For purposes of the Magnuson-Moss Act, a home is not considered to be a consumer product. However, homes *contain* many consumer products. Therefore, the builder's warranty can be affected by the terms of the law. The Magnuson-Moss Act does not require builders to provide a written warranty; however, if a written warranty is provided, the law does require that the document meet certain criteria. Additionally, whether or not the builder provides a warranty on the house itself, the law affects the builder's handling of the manufacturers' warranties on consumer products delivered with the home.

Requirements for the Builder-Backed Warranty

To avoid the complications of complying with Magnuson-Moss, the builder can opt not to provide an express warranty or to exclude all consumer products from coverage. Unfortunately, not providing an express warranty leaves both builder and purchaser without a clear definition of responsibilities, terms, and conditions. This can harm the builder as well as the purchaser. To exclude all consumer products, the builder must define and list those products—a task no one has accomplished with any legal certainty.

Figure 2-4 presents a list of items the Federal Trade Commission (FTC) has identified as consumer products in the home; but courts can add other items if they wish. This list cannot, therefore, be considered definitive. Moreover, if an item in the home is determined by a court to be a consumer product and it was not specifically excluded from coverage by the builder warranty, the warranty document must then comply with Magnuson-Moss requirements.

The simplest way to manage this dilemma—particularly since the Magnuson-Moss disclosure requirements are not hard to meet—is to comply with those requirements in disclosing coverage for all products.

Simple Language and Conspicuous Notice

Clarity of language and conspicuous notice of certain points are required by this law. Consumers often are put off by "fine print" or the legal language used in warranty documents. The FTC's interpretation of the Magnuson-Moss Act requires that warranty information be conveyed in "simple and readily understood" language. Where possible, verbiage such as "henceforth," "hereby," and "parties of the first part" should be replaced with straightforward language. However, the warranty remains a legal document and as such should not become too informal.

Required Details

The Magnuson-Moss Act requires that certain pieces of information be provided in the warranty document. The sample limited warranty in Figure 2-1 presents one way of including this information. (In the descriptions below, the corresponding sections in Figure 2-1 are noted in parentheses.)

Names of Purchasers (Opening Paragraph). The names of the purchasers should be written as shown on the title for the property. This usually means first name, middle initial, last name. If more than one homeowner is to be represented, each name must be written completely and individually (for example, "John J. Smith" and "Mary R. Smith"—not "Mr. and Mrs. John Smith"). As noted before, the signatures at the end of the warranty also must match the way the names appear in the opening paragraph.

Assignability (1). Magnuson-Moss does not require that a warranty be assignable. The law does require that a warranty include a clear statement as to whether or not it is assignable. *Assignability* provides that if the original purchaser sells the home prior to the expiration of the warranty period, the war-

Figure 2-4: Consumer Products

The Federal Trade Commission has provided a list as guidance in identifying items that are considered consumer products under Magnuson-Moss. However, the FTC cautions that this list is neither complete nor definitive; it is only a guideline. The line between what is or is not covered under law as a consumer product has yet to be clearly drawn. In the meantime, prudent builders will conform their documents to existing laws, using the guidance of an attorney and considering the application of warranties in their locales.

The following separate items of equipment are "consumer products" covered by the Magnuson-Moss warranty act when sold as part of a home:

Heating and Ventilation	Appliances	Mechanical/Electrical
Boiler	Refrigerator	Central vacuum system
Heat Pump	Freezer	Smoke detector
Electronic air cleaner	Trash compactor	Fire alarm
Exhaust fan	Range	Fire extinguisher
Thermostat	Oven	Garage door opener
Space heater	Kitchen center	Chimes
Furnace	Dishwasher	Water pump
Air conditioning System	Oven hood	Intercom
Humidifier	Clothes washer	Burglar alarm
	Clothes dryer	Electric meter
Plumbing	Ice Maker	Gas meter
Whirlpool bath		Gas or electric
Garbage disposal		barbecue grill
Water heater		
Water softener		
Sump pump		

Examples of items in these categories that are *not* considered consumer products under the Magnuson-Moss Warranty Act when sold as part of a new home include convectors, light fixtures, lavatories, water closets, sprinkler heads, and miscellaneous items such as cabinets, doors, shelving, windows, and so forth. For consistency, builders treat such items in the same way as consumer items with regard to disclosure. Additional information about consumer items and requirements under the Act is available in publications such as NAHB's *New Home Warranties and the Magnuson-Moss Act: A Primer for Builders.*

ranty automatically is transferred and remains in effect for the new owner. Insured warranties are almost always assignable, whereas builder-backed warranties may not be. In locations where job transfers are common, an assignable warranty may be a useful marketing tool. Buyers concerned about resale will find the fact that their home remains under warranty appealing should they need to move.

Coverage and Exclusions (1, 2, and 7). The statement of coverage and exclusions defines exactly what the builder's warranty covers and what it does not cover. Usually it is most efficient to list any parts of the home that are not covered by the warranty. To avoid any possible misunderstandings between the builder and the customer, exclusions should be clearly and visibly expressed. Damage to items that are not part of the original home or work as purchased from the builder or remodeler, damage to the original home or work caused by normal wear and tear, acts of God, negligence, abuse, change in drainage or failure to maintain drainage, or damage from insects are typical examples of items builders list under exclusions. Use of the property for other than residential purposes or as a rental property also may cause coverage to be terminated. (The list of exclusions may seem lengthy, but the list of what is covered would be much longer.)

Builder's Obligation (3). This clause expresses what the builder will do, generally, if a defect is discovered. Note in particular that the builder agrees "to repair, replace, or pay the reasonable cost of repair or replacement" for any covered defect at no charge to the purchaser. It is wise to mention that the choice among the options is solely that of the builder; this can be important in day-to-day dealings with customers, who may insist that a defective item be replaced when the builder knows a repair is acceptable. In Figure 2-1, the builder's obligation is stated as being limited to the purchase price of the home. To avoid any possible confusion on this point, most builder warranties include a notation in the opening paragraph of the exact amount the buyer paid for the home.

Though not specifically required, written warranty standards are a wise supplement to the warranty coverage outlined and when used should always be referred to in the warranty document itself. Often, the standards are attached to the warranty as "Exhibit A." (In developing written standards, remodelers can refer to the NAHB publication, *Quality Standards for Professional Remodelers.*)

Warranty standards define for the builder and buyer what constitutes a defect and further specifies the method (or choice of methods) to correct the defect. The written standards spell out for the buyer with a fair amount of exactness the point at which the builder becomes liable for a repair. This precise detailing (many standards include an actual measurement) helps establish the buyer's expectations. For this reason, more and more builders are giving this information to customers at the point of sale or sooner. Providing this information early in the process can forestall many disagreements.

Term of Coverage (Opening Paragraph and 1). This section establishes how long the warranty will last and when it starts. Materials and workmanship generally are covered for one year. A few builders offer longer materials and workmanship coverage, but this is still the exception. A two-year systems warranty is becoming more common as builders increasingly duplicate the coverage offered by insured warranty programs. Structural coverage usually extends for ten years. Magnuson-Moss does not dictate how long coverage should be, but rather that the time frames—whatever the builder chooses them to be—must be clearly conveyed to the purchaser.

Coverage usually begins on the date of settlement. One notable exception to this is when the buyer, usually after signing a rental agreement with the builder, occupies the home prior to closing. Under these circumstances, it is normal to enforce the clause that states the warranty begins on the date of closing or the date the purchaser occupies the property, whichever comes first.

Claims Procedures (4). Claims procedures are typically outlined under the owner's obligations. For the majority of builders, claims procedures begin when the purchaser notifies the builder in writing that a problem exists. Emergencies generally are excepted from this requirement and can be reported by telephone. A time limit is set, usually giving the purchaser a thirty-day grace period following expiration of the warranty to report any final items to the builder. This clause often includes a statement that the purchaser must grant the builder access to the home during reasonable hours so that repairs can be performed. It is also common to include a requirement that the purchaser become informed about and provide maintenance for the home. These claims procedures are not part of the Magnuson-Moss requirements.

Consequential Damages (6). If a plumbing leak occurs under warranty, the builder must fix the leak and the drywall damage. If the leak also damages the dining room table and the repair process requires that the water supply to the home be shut off for three days and the family stays at a nearby hotel during that time, consequential, secondary, and incidental damages have been incurred by the homeowner. These costs include the repair of the dining room table, the hotel bill, meals out, putting the family pet in a kennel, and so forth.

The builder's position on reimbursing the homeowner for all or part of these expenses can be influenced by this clause in the warranty. Here again, the Magnuson-Moss Act does not dictate the builder's position, only that it must be clearly stated for the consumer. Most builders state that they do not cover consequential, secondary, or incidental damages. Their obligation is limited to repairing damages to the product that they sold. The customer or the customer's homeowner insurance company is responsible for the cost of other damages.

Unfortunately, this clause cannot prevent the builder from being sued by an angry customer. Also, a court may override the builder's express warranty, holding the builder liable for such damages under concepts of implied warranty.

Some states do not allow exclusion of claims for consequential, secondary, or incidental damages; Magnuson-Moss requires that specific wording in the warranty document call the consumer's attention to that fact. This is an area of state law that each builder should investigate with a qualified attorney.

The difficulty for builders held liable for these types of damages is that the amount of their risk at any given time is unknown. For instance, the builder cannot predict or control the value of items a buyer might move into a new home. In addition, some homeowners may make exaggerated claims for stored property damaged as a result of a leak or other covered item. On the other hand, builders can always make exceptions and agree to cover consequential, secondary, or incidental costs if they believe the circumstances merit extra measures.

Relationship to Implied Warranties (2 and 7). Although Magnuson-Moss prohibits a complete disclaimer of implied warranty on consumer products, a builder's warranty can limit implied warranty coverage to the same time frame as the coverage on the home. Again, because state laws may affect this, notice to that effect must be included. Provided state law does not prohibit disclaimers, the builder can include a disclaimer of implied warranty on parts of the home other than consumer products.

Other Rights. By law, the warranty must include the exact words, "This warranty gives you specific legal rights, and you may also have other rights which vary from state to state."

Availability of Consumer Product Warranties. To ensure that consumers have the opportunity to compare product warranties, the Magnuson-Moss Act requires that manufacturers' warranties be made available for study prior to purchase. Copies of manufacturers' warranties for items such as the furnace, water heater, range, dishwasher, and other consumer products should therefore be available upon request to prospective customers.

The builder can accommodate this requirement in several ways. The manufacturer's warranty can be displayed in the model home on or near each product. A more practical option is to compile a notebook containing the warranties for all consumer products deliverable with the home. This notebook can be kept in a convenient but secure spot in the sales office. A notice can be posted in models referring prospects to the sales office for complete warranty information. (The builder's basic warranty also should be included in the display notebook.)

Custom builders, remodelers, and smaller firms that do not use models can comply with this portion of the law by having available the manufacturers' warranties for those items the customer *selects* from the builder's inventory. Keeping a notebook containing warranties of the consumer products typically selected can save time. Under FTC regulations, manufacturers are obligated to cooperate in supplying these materials. If a telephone call requesting the appropriate documents fails to produce the desired result, a written request mentioning that the literature is needed to comply with the Magnuson-Moss Act should succeed. Displaying warranties for items selected by the buyer from the warehouse or showroom of a supplier becomes the responsibility of the supplier.

For additional details about the Magnuson-Moss Act, builders can obtain a copy of "A Business Person's Guide to Federal Warranty Law" from the U.S. Government Printing office for a small fee. This readable booklet translates the law into everyday language. Another source of information is *New Home Warranties and the Magnuson-Moss Act: A Primer for Builders*, published by NAHB. The full version of the law is reprinted in the latter publication, and is also available from the Federal Trade Commission.

Insured Warranty Programs

Insured warranties offer builders and customers the extra protection of having a third party stand behind the home. Companies such as the Home Owners Warranty Corporation (HOW) provide such protection. HOW also offers a remodelers' warranty policy.

Insured warranty programs establish standards with which participating builders must comply regarding items under one-year, two-year, and ten-year coverage. Should a builder go out of business or a disagreement occur between a builder and a customer, the customer has recourse to a third party. The involvement of a third party also can discourage customers from making excessive claims.

Qualifications and Costs

Builders who participate in insured warranty programs must apply for this coverage. Upon acceptance, builders must maintain specific standards and pass designated inspections of construction or other covered work. Builders pay the premium for the warranty insurance (although this cost generally is considered in the pricing of the home). The warranty insurance policy is issued in the name of the home buyer and commences on the date of the closing.

Premiums are based on the type of coverage selected, the price of the home covered, and sometimes on the builder's volume of business. Routine inspections by a warranty insurance company representative are part of the process of approving each builder for coverage.

Upon closing, a warranty insurance certificate is issued to the homeowner. The warranty certificate includes names, property description, dates, and other specific information just as does the builder warranty. With insured warranty documents, disclosures remain subject to Magnuson-Moss requirements.

Warranty Support

Insured warranty programs almost always include dispute resolution procedures. If a homeowner and builder disagree on a warranty matter, the warranty company will arrange for informal dispute settlement using a neutral third party.

If a builder goes out of business or for some other reason is unable to provide a repair, the homeowner can turn to the warranty company for assistance. Under some circumstances, the homeowner must pay a deductible or a filing fee to the warranty company to have a claim processed. The program information and printed standards supplied to buyers through the builder cover these points and should be carefully studied by builder before a final choice of the insurance program is made.

Types of Insured Warranty Coverage

Insured warranty programs can vary in some details. Most programs will offer three types of coverage, however: one-year for materials and workmanship, two-year for systems defects, and ten-year for structural defects.

One-year Materials and Workmanship Coverage. The warranty company establishes standards with which builders must comply regarding this portion of the warranty coverage. The customer reports warranty items in writing to the builder, sending a copy of the request to the warranty company. The builder inspects the defects and provides repairs, administering the work of subcontractors where appropriate. The cost of warranty repairs are the builder's (or the sub's) responsibility. If the builder cannot or will not provide repairs meeting the published standards of the warranty program, the customer can file a claim with the warranty company. If the warranty company agrees with the customer, the company arranges to provide the work and resolves the issue with the builder.

Two-year Systems Coverage. Second-year coverage is provided for mechanical systems with the exception of fixtures (such as chandeliers, faucets, sinks, and so forth). Again, the customer reports the items to the builder, who screens claims and provides needed repairs to bring the item within standards as published by the warranty company. If the builder is unwilling or unable to perform the needed repair, the same enforcement steps apply.

Structural Coverage. Insured warranty coverage for structural damages differ somewhat from the other types of coverage. The warranty company bears the financial risk of the cost of structural repairs. Usually, coverage for structural defects extends for at least ten years. With some policies, the builder may be responsible for covering the first one or two years, with years three through ten covered by the warranty company. With other policies, the warranty company covers structural defects from the date of closing through year ten. In either situation, coverage begins immediately for the homeowner.

If coverage of structural defects is provided, the warranty certificate will include specific language describing what kinds of items constitute "major structural defects" and what items do not. Major structural defects generally involve load-bearing portions of the home which are sufficiently damaged or defective to render the home "unsafe, unsanitary, or otherwise unlivable."

As with the other types of coverage, the homeowner initially submits the problem to the builder for screening. If the builder's inspection confirms the problem, the claim is forwarded to the warranty company for its inspection and action. If the builder and customer disagree, the warranty company becomes involved and assists in resolving the issue.

Extensions of Coverage. Warranty insurance companies may offer extensions of coverage on structural defects to buyers of homes built by qualifying builders. Such extensions typically are offered in five-year increments. The warranty company contacts the homeowner near the end of the original period of coverage; if the homeowner elects to extend coverage, he or she assumes responsibility for the premiums and coverage continues uninterrupted.

Builder Literature and Documents

The sales agreements used by the builder should refer to the type and length of warranty coverage that will be provided. The sales agreement should also note that the warranty will be provided at settlement. Even though the complete, signed warranty document is not delivered at the time the contract (or sales agreement) is signed, a specimen copy of the warranty, including the written standards, should be provided to the customer. This step is fundamental to educating the customer about warranty and establishing accurate expectations.

It may be tempting to use the warranty as another sales tool, but builders must be cautious about making or implying promises that may go unfulfilled, particularly on matters that are open to interpretation. Sales and marketing literature should promise no more than the warranty will provide. Vague, general statements create vulnerability for the builder; they may lead to misunderstandings, disagreements and additional, unnecessary expenses.

A Legal Reminder

Warranty laws vary, sometimes considerably, from state to state. For example, the state of New Jersey requires that builders provide insured warranties. In California, a conspicuous notice must advise buyers that they relinquish specific rights by agreeing to a dispute resolution clause. Moreover, the purchaser must initial this clause separately within the document to confirm acceptance of the clause.

As with any legal document, builders should consult with an attorney for specific details and conditions that may apply locally, influencing the language and content of the warranty. Builders also should make every attempt to stay informed about new legislation or court actions that may impact their warranties. Examples of unclear obligations include the fire-retardant treated plywood, radon, and "blue water" issues. Questions about who is liable in cases involving these issues (and the extent of that liability) will be resolved during the next several years. As these issues are resolved—and as other issues surface—the resulting case law and precedents will significantly affect builders. One way to stay informed about current developments is to participate in programs sponsored by local builder and remodeler associations.

WHAT CUSTOMERS EXPECT

When customers pay a lot of money for something, they expect few problems with the product. If problems do occur, customers expect them to be corrected immediately. Further, customers feel that the company they purchased the item from should sincerely regret their inconvenience—and say so.

Anything short of attentive, courteous service disappoints the customer by putting the buying experience out of alignment with expectations. When the product purchased is a home, a customer's expectations are often so elaborate it would take an entire scrapbook to compile them.

The Customer's Mental Scrapbook

The "mental scrapbook" of expectations sets the context within which each builder succeeds or fails to satisfy the customer. Every customer has such a scrapbook; it is in effect, the cumulative product of that person's housing experiences.

Every home buyer has lived somewhere else before. In each home, in childhood or adulthood, whether single-family, apartment, farmhouse, or tent, the person formed likes and dislikes. The homes of friends and family, houses seen on television or in movies, and homes pictured in magazines all contribute ideas to the mental scrapbook. These ideas can be categorized under headings such as "must have," "can't stand," "prefer to avoid," and "hope to have." Features included might be anything: large windows, a three-car garage, a great view, a quiet neighborhood, or walk-in closets. When talking with a remodeler, a customer

40

usually is changing an existing home to coincide more closely with this mental scrapbook.

Customers shop for a new home or remodeling design with these expectations fixed more or less clearly in their minds. Some customers bring a specific list of what they want when they walk into the sales office or meet with a remodeler. Others have only a vague idea of what they are seeking, presenting the "I'll know it when I see it" attitude. It is important to remember that these latter folks have a mental scrapbook just as potent as the former group: they simply have not formalized it.

Tradeoffs Are Expected

Whatever the customer's budget, it is rare for any buyer to find the exact combination of characteristics sought—price, location, plus specific features—all in one product. A great deal of what is in the scrapbook may be dream or fantasy; features may have been added haphazardly, often without regard to cost. Most buyers realize this and expect there will be some tradeoffs, some give and take. The buyer may need to choose between the preferred school district and a short drive to work, an eat-in kitchen and wood windows, a main floor master suite and a walk-out site for the home, the ceramic floor or new cabinets for the remodeled kitchen.

Builders discover and work through the customer's expectations about the physical product through conversations, by displaying models, and by providing plans and written information listing product specifications. In effect, the builder edits the customer's mental scrapbook, helping to sift through the dreams and fantasies to arrive at a mutually acceptable reality.

Details are explored, priorities set, costs adjusted. If there are too many "gives" and not enough "takes," the customer may decide "to keep on looking" or "wait a while longer." The weighing and balancing of one feature against another will continue until the customer selects a home or completes decisions on a remodeling assignment.

After a customer locates the combination of factors that, within budget, will most closely match the mental scrapbook, an agreement is signed and construction proceeds. For example: A new-home customer has toured the model and is aware that the master bath has a walk-in shower. If a whirlpool tub was in the "hope to have" category of this customer's scrapbook, he or she may ask the builder about having the plan changed, balance the cost against other desired features, consider the budget, and decide not to have it installed. After moving in, the customer will not resent the builder because the tub is not there.

After discussing the pricing for several types of windows and reviewing two different cabinet layouts for the new kitchen, a remodeler's customer may select the less expensive windows and the cabinet plan that provides more storage. During the discussion, and in making the choice, the customer's initial expectations of the remodeling job have been adjusted.

Customers' expectations are not limited to the physical items included with the product. They extend to what customers expect from the builder's warranty service commitment. These expectations about service are not left at the closing table and they do not cease to exist when the final check is written. Customer expectations move right into the home or co-exist with the remodeling project. When the customer is living with the project, expectations become very active and begin to affect the relationship with the builder. Each time the customer requests service, comparisons between service expectations and the reality are inevitable.

Until recently, not much has been done to adjust the customer's expectations about warranty service. The customer expects "good" service. The builder intends to provide "good" service. Both parties mistakenly assume that they understand each other. But unless the two parties have explored and agreed upon a set of characteristics defining "good" service, their two definitions probably will not match. Many of the differences will show up later, possibly in unpleasant exchanges.

In the past, the necessity of discussing this information went unrecognized. Warranty details typically were delivered to the customer at settlement. Seldom, if ever, did customers read through the materials or ask questions.

Developing the materials needed and training staff—or learning yourself—to accomplish this task well takes time and work. Many builders have good intentions of taking this important step, but find it difficult to set aside the time to develop the program. Ironically, however, it can take yet more time and energy to settle disagreements with customers.

Bear in mind, customers do not usually make choices about warranty. Builders generally do not offer standard versus optional, upgraded warranties. The warranty is just something that comes with the house. There is nothing to select, no price difference to balance against other features.

Many aspects of warranty service are therefore invisible at the start. The emotional tone of service must be experienced. The cheerfulness or friendliness of the service manager and repair technicians cannot be conveyed convincingly on paper to customers. Appointments cannot be kept until they have been made. Service personnel demonstrate their knowledge when there is something to be knowledgeable about. Besides, builders and customers may be reluctant to talk about repairs when everyone hopes there will never need to be any. And bringing up such a "negative" subject in the midst of the sale certainly is not something salespeople jump at the chance to do.

Builders who fail to discuss and adjust their customers' service expectations leave customer satisfaction to chance. Keeping in mind that the customer's mental scrapbook is a collection of wishes and dreams not subject to the test of practical reality, chance favors the customer expecting more than the builder will deliver. When this occurs, the builder does not have a satisfied customer. The builder has missed an opportunity to increase a positive reputation and help the business prosper.

Even a custom builder cannot completely change warranty and service procedures to accommodate the preferences of each customer. However, every builder can inform each customer about the company's warranty service program. Adjusting customer expectations regarding the physical features of a property occurs as a natural part of the selling process. No builder would simply say, "the house will have a master bath." No remodeler would stop at saying, "the new kitchen will have windows." To prevent the serious problems that arise from discrepancies between service expectations and reality, builders need to make their warranty service methods and standards as clear as they make their product.

What Expectations Need Adjusting?

All customers consider five aspects of warranty service in forming an opinion of the builder's performance: process, warranty standards and maintenance, timeliness, quality, and attitude.

These five aspects will apply whether the builder specializes in high-end custom products, starter homes, kitchen and bath remodeling, or deck installations. Builders must first establish feasible expectations in each area before they can educate and then satisfy the customer.

Process

This aspect of warranty service affects all the others. As with the many other tasks that, assembled, form a builders business, warranty service often benefits when its many steps are organized into an efficient, streamlined process. The process should support repair activities while also considering customer needs and desires.

Convenience. Understandably, the customers' first choice would be never to have any problems with their new or remodeled home. Most customers realize that in a product as large as a home, a few details may need attention along the way. A warranty process that makes it easy for the customer to obtain this attention can prevent frustration and disagreements.

Get it in Writing. Many builders ask homeowners to report non-emergency items in writing. Most customers consider this practice inconvenient, and many customers feel it is intended to discourage their obtaining deserved attention.

Indeed it does require more work and time than picking up the phone; but builders have fair and substantial reasons for requiring reports in writing. A builder's office staff can spend hours each week engaged in recording lists by phone. Inaccuracies easily occur, and conversations wander off the subject, using valuable time that could be put to better use screening and processing service requests.

Also, a harried and frustrated office employee may finally receive one too many calls and respond in a curt or offensive way. The umpteenth time an angry homeowner asks why service has not been forthcoming on items called in a week ago, the employee may scream into the innocent homeowner's ear, "Because I spend all my time on the phone listening to you people complain!" This kind of exchange indicates that the builder's procedures are not working to help the customer *or* the employee.

To gain the cooperation of customers in sending written warranty claims, builders need simply call attention to legitimate reasons for the policy and point out genuine benefits to the customer. To say, "That's our policy" is not sufficient; "That's what our warranty says" also will not do it. Two good reasons are increased accuracy and the ability of the builder's staff to process service requests more efficiently, therefore providing faster, more complete service. By far the best reason is the protection this step provides. Written notice to the builder, with a copy retained for the customer's records, documents for both parties which items were reported and when. This method is ultimately more convenient for the customer than calling items in and hoping the report is taken down accurately, will not be lost, and that someone will have time to respond to it.

Many customers will accept a requirement to "put it in writing" more readily if the builder provides a simple form that can be filled out. The process of writing a business letter can intimidate those who do not do it often. For others, having to write business letters at home may simply be an unpleasant task. An advantage to the builder is that a form can standardize the information received with the homeowner's list—phone numbers, closing date, model, job number and so on (see the sample service request forms in chapter 6).

Scheduled Warranty Contacts. How often do customers contact the builder for service? If the builder does not promote a planned schedule of communications, customers will follow their own expectations. Left to their own choices, some will send daily or weekly letters; others will move in and never be heard from again. A suggested schedule of routine communications shows the customer there is order and organization to warranty service. This can help to keep the prolific writers under control, and balance service between them and those less likely to make contact. Whatever the builder's position on this aspect of service, the customer has a right to be informed of it.

Inspections and Access. Most builders want to inspect the items reported for warranty attention. This allows the builder to screen the problem, determine whether it is a legitimate warranty item, and evaluate whether it is a serious or recurring item that needs further investigation. If an inspection will be a normal step in obtaining service, the customer should be made aware of this and the inspection scheduled promptly.

Access to the home must be granted for inspections and for repair work. Whether access can be arranged by appointment only or by the homeowner providing the builder with a key should be discussed and settled *before* service is needed. The builder who has possession of a homeowner's key also has both a responsibility and a potential liability right along with it. Many builders accept the risks involved rather than inconvenience the customer by requiring that the homeowner be present when work is performed.

Scheduling Service Work. Every builder seems to have at least one customer who can say with a straight face, "I work from 5:30 a.m. until 9:45 p.m. every day of the year, including Sundays and Christmas. I never take lunch. Your service people will have to come at 9:58 p.m. on New Year's Day. That's the only time I can stay home to let them in." This discussion can be avoided if the builder volunteers, before the subject is brought up by the customer, that service hours are 8:00 a.m. until 4:30 p.m., Monday through Friday.

Flexibility may be desirable in some areas, but not in this one. Builders who provide service at odd hours are providing service without supervision, without reasonable access to other personnel for answers to questions, and often without ready availability of parts and materials. If repairs are performed during evening and weekend hours, service technicians may become involved in long conversations with family members who are usually not at home during normal hours. This can greatly increase service costs (and ultimately product cost) while delaying attention for other homeowners. Maintaining a staff and a collection of subcontractors willing to comply with irregular work hours is not easily done, especially over the long term. Once the precedent of irregular hours is set, it is difficult to change—and more difficult to maintain.

Many procedures and policies about which customers complain have valid reasons, but builders cannot expect homeowners to know these reasons. A few moments spent covering procedures and the logic behind them will usually gain the customer's cooperation.

Warranty Standards and Maintenance

Is the builder fair in determining what will be fixed? Customers sometimes are displeased with specific standards applied to judge their warranty requests. "That's not acceptable" may sound like a common remark. Although the building industry and an individual builder may agree that a particular defect falls within an acceptable standard, the customer may have a different opinion. This type of disagreement can be doubly difficult to resolve when the offending defect is obvious.

Car manufacturers have tied their warranties to measures that are not open to interpretation: 50,000 miles or five years, 30,000 miles or 24 months, 16 feet or 12 seconds, etc. Customers may not like the specific time frame or mileage limit, but they cannot misunderstand it. Interpretations are not a problem.

Builders too often rely on the overworked phrase, "industry standards." The term may be quoted to a homeowner as an explanation of why an item does not qualify for service from the builder: "Well, it meets industry standards." To a customer who has just found a problem in a new home, industry standards sounds a lot like an excuse drawn from the builder's rich and imaginative collection of ways to avoid responsibility. To some homeowners, "industry standards," seem to be a mysterious set of privately held principles known only to the initiated and subject to change at the whim of the builder.

Most customers are neither familiar nor comfortable with industry standards. They express this through comments such as, "It's the principle of the matter," a sure sign that expectations about being treated fairly are not being met.

Builders are quite capable of defining for customers the standards that are used to screen warranty items. Standards should be written using language that an individual not devoted to the construction industry can readily understand. They should specify the point at which any given defect is considered serious enough to qualify for repair or replacement. Stopping at this point, however, leaves half the task undone.

Many new homeowners are disappointed to discover after moving in that some items need maintenance from the first day, and that maintenance is provided by the homeowner, not the home builder. This can be especially difficult for buyers who are accustomed to rental housing, where maintenance attention is provided by a landlord. The shift to ownership carries a shift in responsibilities.

Once reminded of this basic principle, most buyers acknowledge the logic and fairness of it. The next step is to define the specific details that separate maintenance from warranty obligations, calling attention to examples of specific maintenance responsibilities of the homeowner. It is not enough to state that "normal maintenance will be provided by the homeowner." A common homeowner response to this is, "I realize the builder does not provide maintenance. But after I paid $X for this house, the caulking, painting, grouting, roof, plumbing, concrete, and so forth should last longer than this."

Once again, the best time to answer this question is before it is even asked by the customer. The builder should volunteer information and specific examples of items that will require maintenance. Many customers move into a new home or accept completion of remodeling expecting that they will not have to do anything to care for it for a year or longer. Frequently, customers find they have spent more money than they intended, and some spend more than they should. For people who are struggling to pay for something, repair and maintenance costs take on even greater meaning. Builders must work hard from the start to keep customers realistic about warranty repairs and home maintenance.

Timeliness

Builders should respond quickly to warranty requests. Builders cannot fax repair technicians in and out of homes, but today's customer uses the time it takes to respond as a primary criterion for evaluating service performance. The builder can supply service vans that sparkle, well-trained, uniformed personnel who speak five languages fluently, gold-edged business cards, and brilliant repair work—but if the repair work is not done until six months after the items were reported, the builder may as well not have bothered with the other glorious details.

Just as everyone agrees service should be "good," all parties believe service should be "quick." Again, the problem comes when one defines "quick." The homeowner may define it as "same day" whereas subcontractors may define it as "sometime this calendar quarter." The builder must consider all aspects of service and set a reasonable time frame.

The temptation to quote an average number of days should be resisted. It is far better to acclimate the customer to a realistic but slightly longer time estimate than to quote an average and have the service end up on the slow side of that number.

Consider two builders, each enthusiastic about service. One promises that warranty response time will be ten days, but delivers the service in thirteen days. The customer is disappointed. The other builder promises a response time of fifteen days, and provides service in thirteen. Both homeowners have experienced the same thirteen-day response time. But the second customer will be pleasantly surprised instead of disappointed.

The principle here is to promise what can consistently be delivered, to set a standard that can be met or exceeded. However, there is a limit to applying this principle: imagine a builder who promises a service response time of no more than 180 days. Even if service is completed in "only" 173 days, the customer probably will not be impressed. The typical response time for builders is thirty days. Therefore, meeting a thirty-day service deadline will not distinguish the organization. The shorter the time frame the better; but the promise should not exceed the reality.

When delays occur for legitimate reasons, customers will expect the builder to keep them informed. Customers want reassurance that the matter has not been forgotten or lost. Most homeowners are very understanding about back-ordered parts and materials that are difficult to obtain. They simply want to know that someone is still attending to the repair. A phone call every week or two or a postcard, including, if possible, an expected service delivery date, will mitigate any negativity.

Emergency Situations. Customers, quite reasonably, expect the builder to have anticipated the possibility of emergency situations and to have a system for correcting them immediately. Planning ahead makes such problems seem routine and they will cause less panic. Emergency procedures need to be carefully and accurately explained to the homeowner. From time to time, the builder should check emergency systems to confirm that reasonably fast "after hours" responses are available from critical subcontractors—heating, plumbing, and electrical.

Along with developing emergency instructions for customers, builders should consider under what circumstances, if any, they will pay for hotel accommodations for customers who must stay out of their homes. Many warranties specify that the builder does not pay for incidental damages; however, some extenuating circumstances can change the builder's opinion on this subject. It is helpful to have planned ahead for such contingencies, to avoid making impulsive decisions under pressure.

Quality

Is the repair work effective in correcting the original problem without causing any new ones? Is the work complete?

A builder can adjust the customer's expectations to so low a level that the customer simply gives up, thinking "There is no point in telling 'Build & Remodel, Inc.' about these problems; they won't fix them properly anyway." A builder may unintentionally end up with a very cynical, pessimistic customer. With that attitude, the customer will no doubt be able to find problems: expecting them and watching for them, he or she may not tell the builder, but will probably share the information with friends.

A builder adjusts the customer's expectations first with words and then with actions. The adage that actions speak louder than words holds true with customers. Results make a more lasting impression than lofty promises. A positive long-term service image is built on what actually happens to the customer. Procedures may be convenient, standards may be fair, and service may be fast; but if the repair is not a repair, both builder and customer have lost.

Providing an ineffective, sloppy, three-visit repair destroys the customer's respect for a builder's service program. Examples of ineffective repairs are easy to find: the plumber fixes the leaky faucet, but the toolbox scratches the countertop; the repairman arrives to adjust a sticking door and tracks mud on the off-white carpet; having missed the first appointment, the drywall sub shows up with insufficient material to repair the damage from the roof leak; the window supplier sends a service person out to adjust a window that's difficult to open, only to discover that the framing is the real problem, and so forth. This "three ring circus" atmosphere is avoidable if the service people handling the repair work

- understand exactly what is wrong and what caused it,
- identify who can correct the problem as well as any necessary follow-up work (such as drywall repair and repainting after a plumbing leak),
- communicate clearly and accurately all the information the repair people need, and
- confirm that the intended repair was completed within the assigned time frame.

Customers are reasonable in expecting that someone who can build a home or complete a remodeling assignment will be able to stand behind their work. Parts of the warranty system, such as the inspection step, exist to support this goal. These steps will all seem justified to the customer if the resulting repairs are satisfactory.

Attitude

Are service personnel pleasant? Customers will forgive many things—lack of heat in the middle of a freezing night, a defective light fixture, a lost warranty list, even a missed appointment. But few customers ever forget or forgive a service manager or technician who is discourteous or belligerent. To the customer, the builder is the one who sold the problem along with the product. It is unacceptable for the builder or builder's representative to be angry with the customer for finding a problem.

Along with effective, timely repairs, customers want courtesy, respect, and thoughtful consideration. The personal nature of the contact between service personnel and the homeowner requires that personalities be taken into account when service assignments are made.

Attitude is communicated to the customer not only by actions and words, but by body language as well. Posture, tone of voice, gestures, and facial expressions all send clear messages. Service personnel must be able to put their personal problems or professional disagreements aside when dealing with customers. An enthusiastic, positive approach will favorably impress customers.

These subtle aspects of warranty service are important to the customer's ultimate satisfaction with the home, and contribute to the builder's reputation. It is difficult to convey convincing information about attitude to a customer who has not yet experienced the builder's service performance. Customers' expectations will develop based on the behavior of a builder's other employees. Pleasant, enthusiastic sales and construction personnel will lead customers to expect the same qualities in warranty service personnel; however, if sales and construction personnel have left a negative impression, warranty service staff will have to work harder to change that image.

Unique Warranty Strategies

Some markets require special warranty strategies. But the search for an unusual approach offers a dangerous temptation to ignore the basics. Creating a new way of handling warranty may be more exciting, but working hard at the basics is essential to success. Arranging flamboyant programs without the support of solid performance on the fundamentals is like trying to frost a cake before baking it. The builder who delivers an elaborate thank-you gift a month after the customer moves in might be surprised to learn that the customers would rather have their warranty items corrected promptly.

If the basics are in place, developing an unusual warranty strategy can add excitement to service work and can bring long-term marketing benefits. An excellent place to begin is to study the customers: Who are they? What is the nature of their lifestyle and financial circumstances? Would they be interested in "co-producing" service?

For some markets, low price is essential. Those customers may be willing to participate in warranty service in exchange for that benefit. Some builders have carried this concept one step further and have been very successful with a warranty savings account program. A savings account is established in the customer's name and held until the warranty expires. If the customer handles the warranty items, the funds go to the customer at the end of the warranty. If the customer contacts the builder for warranty attention, it is promptly provided and an hourly charge is deducted from the savings account. If a balance remains at the end of the warranty period, it is given to the customer. This financial incentive minimizes the nuisance items that typically pass through a warranty office. The cost to the builder is very reasonable compared to regular warranty service. This approach works well with buyers who are willing to contact subs or even do minor repairs themselves in exchange for the money involved. In managing a program like this, dependable subs are critical!

For another market, luxury treatment may be a strategy. For high-end product, warranty service might include many generous extras such as paint touch-up after the owners move in, and coverage of some "maintenance" items such as touch-up caulking, sealing grout, repair of normal shrinkage cracks in drywall, recoating wood flooring, sealing decks, leveling a/c pads, filling settled areas, or even an aggressive replacement policy for plant material.

For this high-end market, some builders sell service extras through the warranty office. Luxury buyers can choose from a list of repairs and pay the builder to perform them. This procedure helps provide services desired by the market while keeping such activities distinct from standard warranty services.

Remodelers might list paid follow-up procedures at the end of the warranty, such as resealing decks they installed as part of routine service. Such services can be offered for a modest price; and the customer contact provides an excellent opportunity to prospect for new work, such as enclosing the same deck, other work that might be desired in the home, or referrals to other potential customers.

Ideas for new warranty strategies may arise from geographic location, buyer demographics, or product characteristics. Builders considering their target markets can ask:

- What is important to these buyers?
- What special warranty features might attract this market?
- How can we differentiate ourselves from our competitors?

Finding and implementing the answers to these questions can distinguish the builder, drawing customer attention, loyalty, and referrals.

Whether a builder creates a unique approach to warranty or simply focuses on doing a fine job with the basics, making a concentrated effort to educate the customer about what to expect during the warranty period allows the builder the best opportunity to satisfy those same customers. All customers expect good service, and smart builders define that term precisely for their buyers.

4

EDUCATING THE CUSTOMER

Customer satisfaction with warranty service is the byproduct of forthright education that begins in the sales office and continues through the transition from buyer to owner. As seen in chapter 3, a significant amount of information needs to be conveyed to the customer in order to create and maintain realistic expectations. This is best begun during the sales process.

Starting Early

Adjusting customer expectations will be much easier if it is done *before* the customer makes final decisions. If positioned well by sales personnel, the builder's warranty and service program can be one of the reasons a prospect decides to do business with the company.

The complexity and volume of information about the warranty, procedures, standards, and maintenance responsibilities demand written back-up. The excitement of the new home purchase can motivate the customer to read through this somewhat dry literature if it is supplied early. On the other hand, a customer who is just about to move is unlikely to read it.

Customer questions can be discussed calmly if they are addressed early. When questions do not surface until the parties reach the closing table, everyone feels pressured and resolving issues is awkward at best. If unspoken questions are not addressed until after the customer moves in, the customer may end up feeling that the product and service were intentionally misrepresented. Although this is not usually the case, if the customer believes it, it may as well be true. Encouraging customers to read through warranty materials and ask questions early gives the impression that the builder or remodeler has the customer's best interest in mind.

Training Sales Staff About Warranty

For the builder to take full advantage of the opportunity to create realistic expectations in a customer, the sales staff must appreciate the importance of the task and understand what points must be reviewed. Salespeople must also recognize when to ask other company personnel for assistance in answering customer questions about warranty. Making up an answer to a customer's warranty question is not conducive to long-term customer satisfaction. A salesperson's interpretation of a standard or procedure will be remembered by the customer. Although contracts typically state that "all agreements are in writing," verbal commitments seem to have a half-life of 800 years and can haunt a builder forever.

Training the sales staff to present solid information about warranty can be accomplished swiftly and easily. Initial training can be as simple as a homework assignment and a couple of meetings between sales and warranty personnel. Long-term, regular communication between sales and warranty staffs will keep each group sensitive to the needs of the other and provides a forum to resolve issues or questions.

For small-volume builders who "wear all the hats," coordination between staffs may not be an issue; but training *themselves* to think "warranty" when in a sales setting is just as important. Particularly in smaller companies, builders may be tempted to answer warranty questions "on the fly" rather than taking time out to focus on specific training. In the long term, however, an organized approach will pay off in more consistent treatment of customers by staff.

The first step in training is to ask the sales staff to read and become familiar with the warranty, standards, maintenance information, and all procedures and forms. The paragraph in the sales agreement that addresses warranty should be included on the list of materials to study (See Figure 4-1). Sales staff should be encouraged to jot notes in the margins or highlight points that need clarification, as will make their subsequent meeting with the warranty staff more productive. This is an excellent time to recommend that warranty staff also reread these documents. It is not unusual to discover that warranty personnel have not reviewed this material in a long time.

Figure 4-1: Sample Warranty Clause from Purchase and Sales Agreement

LIMITED WARRANTY: SELLER DISCLAIMS AND PURCHASERS WAIVE THE IMPLIED WARRANTY OF HABITABILITY THAT THE RESIDENCE WILL BE FREE OF DEFECTS AND WILL BE FIT FOR ITS INTENDED PURPOSE AS A HOME. Seller and Purchasers agree to execute at closing Builder, Inc.'s Limited Warranty Agreement. After closing, all claims, rights and remedies of Seller and Purchasers arising out of this contract and Seller's construction and sale of the residence and any consumer products in the residence shall be limited to those set forth in the Limited Warranty Agreement, which is incorporated herein by reference. SUCH WARRANTY AGREEMENT IS INSTEAD OF ALL OTHER WARRANTIES OF HABITABILITY OR WORKMANLIKE CONSTRUCTION AND ANY OTHER EXPRESS OR IMPLIED WARRANTIES TO WHICH PURCHASERS MIGHT BE ENTITLED. This Agreement shall survive delivery of the deed referred to in paragraph (*) hereof. Purchasers acknowledge that they have received copies of a specimen of the Builder, Inc. Limited Warranty Agreement and Exhibit A, Construction Standards for Warranty.

This sample is provided for purposes of illustration only. When developing or revising warranty documents or other legal documents, always have them reviewed by an attorney qualified for the state(s) in which they will be used.

The next step is to arrange a meeting between sales and warranty staff. At the meeting, review the general process of handling warranty items. Salespeople do not need enough detailed information to handle warranty claims, but they should know enough to answer typical customer questions, such as "Why does everything have to be submitted in writing?" Staff questions about specific details in the warranty documents also can be answered in this meeting.

This is an excellent time to suggest that all involved create or review their personal "knowledge network" checklist (see Figure 4-2). Each employee can serve the customer only to the extent of his or her knowledge, assisted by available staff contacts for additional input. If an area of a knowledge network needs strengthening, no employee should feel uncomfortable saying, "I have a question . . ." or "Something came up the other day I've never heard of before . . . ."

Between the first and second meeting, if possible, each participant should visit a competitor in an effort to learn more about their service programs. Exploring the product, prices, warranty information, and attitude of competitors can result in increased

Figure 4-2: Knowledge Network Worksheet

Knowledge Network for Customer Service

Identify areas where strengthening your background will improve your customer service. Add topics to customize your network for your particular area and product.

Topic   Comment

_____   _____

_____   _____

_____   _____

Extended Community:

Local political issues:

Local economic conditions: _____

Government services:

    Voter registration: _____

    Car registration: _____

    Driver's license: _____

Transportation:

    Highways: _____

    Bus: _____

    Taxi: _____

    Airport: _____

Utilities:

    Electric: _____

    Gas: _____

    Water: _____

    Sewer: _____

Cable TV: _____

Newspapers: _____

Libraries: _____

Museums: _____

Schools: _____

Day care: _____

Medical and dental: _____

(continued on next page)

(continued from previous page)

Banking: _____

Religious facilities: _____

Recreation: _____

Shopping: _____

Builder's Company Background:

Experience: _____

Company size: _____

Production: _____

Philosophy: _____

Housing Community:

Demographics: _____

Homeowner Association: _____

Amenities: _____

Future of Area: _____

Product:

Floor plans: _____

Square footage: _____

Features: _____

Optional items, upgrades: _____

Available plan changes: _____

Special needs: _____

Elevations: _____

Lot sizes: _____

Lot characteristics: _____

Construction Process:

Colors, Lighting: _____

Time limits for changes: _____

Visits to site: _____

Foundation: _____

Waterproof/perimeter drain: _____

Framing: _____

Roof: _____

(continued on next page)

(continued from previous page)

Exterior trim: _____

Exterior finish: _____

Grading: _____

Landscaping: _____

Floor covering: _____

Hardware: _____

Lights: _____

Homeowner Walk-Through:

Scheduling: _____

Time required: _____

Purposes: _____

Conducted by (person): _____

Time to complete list: _____

Access to home for work: _____

Follow-up to confirm: _____

Warranty Coverage and Service:

Types of coverage: _____

Self-insured or outside insurance: _____

Extended coverage: _____

Duration of coverages: _____

Limitations on coverage: _____

Standards: _____

Zoning Department: _____

Building Department: _____

Suppliers and Contractors: _____

pride and confidence, stimulate new ideas, or in some cases, awaken increased efforts to improve.

If a builder senses any defensiveness among staff members about the standards the company uses in making warranty decisions, having staff take a short exercise comparing several programs may increase their comfort level (see Figure 4-3). It is vital that builder personnel feel their warranty is fair and reasonable. By confirming in their own minds that other builders also set similar (often identical) limits, their confidence will increase.

At the second meeting, the employees who visited a competitor can share their impressions. This provides a valuable perspective for all involved. How do the companies' service programs compare? If the nearest competitor has extended their materials and workmanship warranty to two years, the builder will want to be aware of this.

Also on the agenda for this second meeting are any questions that have come up since the first meeting. As warranty information works its way into the sales presentation, the sales staff may need clarification of some points or have some insights to contribute.

One person on the warranty staff should be designated to be primarily responsible for answering questions from salespeople This person must have the knowledge and authority to answer warranty questions for the company in an honest, straightforward way without alienating potential customers or buyers who are under contract.

Finally, the builder should assess how often and under what circumstances any future meetings will take place. For one organization, a one-hour monthly meeting may be sufficient, for

Figure 4-3: Standards Comparison

Compare the terms and standards of Builder, competitor and insured warranties.

	Builder			Insured
	A	B	C	
Exterior paint fades				
Concrete drive cracks				
Backfill settles				
Drywall nail pops				
Transferable to new owner				
Homeowner changes drainage				
Plumbing leak				
Plumbing clog				
Broken window				
Uneven floor				

another, a weekly visit by the warranty manager to one sales office each week might work best.

However it is accomplished, some ongoing communication between sales people and warranty personnel needs to be established. Salespeople have a hard time understanding why warranty must sometimes say "no" to a customer; warranty staff have difficulty empathizing with the salesperson's tendency to want to say "yes" to any customer demand. Regular contact helps keep both teams in touch with reality and sensitive to the other's point of view. This sensitivity is vital to avoiding the sense of opposition that easily can develop.

Attitude

A trained sales staff will have an appreciation of the complexities of warranty work, confidence in the company's system, and pride in the quality of the overall service program. Their underlying faith in the program will be communicated to prospects not only in words but through the salesperson's body language, that silent two-thirds of the communication that takes place between people. Unless the sales staff sincerely believes in the value and fairness of the builder's warranty program, they will not be effective in presenting it to buyers.

Their appreciation of the customer's right and need to be aware of standards and procedures will encourage the sales staff to present the necessary information and assist the customer to recognize its importance. Some customers will accept warranty information immediately and comprehend the principles involved. Other customers will be confused by it and may question many seemingly trivial details. Patience and willingness to discuss will pay off. If the salesperson needs assistance he or she should be completely comfortable in asking the warranty manager or other designated individual to talk with the customer.

Support Tools

No sales professional should be expected to memorize and recite the intricacies of warranty standards to a customer. Even were this possible, no customer would be able to absorb or remember all of them. The job of the salesperson is to present the information with pride and confidence, emphasize its importance and assist the customer in understanding it. Several items can be used to support the salesperson's presentation.

Warranty Specimen

Specimen copies of the warranty itself begin the list of items that support the sales team's efforts. Although this is just the beginning of what is needed, it is the most legal in tone and appearance.

Warranty Standards

If the builder provides an insured warranty, literature supplied by the insurance company will explain the minimum standards to which the builder has agreed (see chapter 2). Some builders prefer to write their own, in which case the builder also specifies the standards. While the measurements involved change only slightly (if at all) from one set of standards to another, the wording can vary from highly technical to chatty. The personality of the builder and the tone the builder wishes to convey will determine the style. Some standards are presented on charts, others in paragraph form. Whatever the format, it must be designed to make individual topics easy to locate. Tiny print and obscure titles will discourage the customer. The wording should be as precise as possible and each point should be phrased in a positive tone. Figures 4-4 and 4-5 present additional information regarding standards, along with sample wording.

Figure 4-4: Possible Topics for Written Warranty Standards

1. Heating (see Figure 4-5)	16. Countertops
2. Air conditioning	17. Appliances
3. Plumbing	18. Telephone jacks
4. Electrical	19. Fireplace
5. Insulation	20. Concrete
6. Drywall	21. Crawl space
7. Sub floor	22. Roof
8. Paint and stain/interior	23. Gutters and downspouts
9. Paint and stain/exterior	24. Louvers and vents
10. Windows and screens	25. Siding
11. Wood trim	26. Stucco
12. Doors	27. Exterior trim
13. Hardware	28. Garage overhead door
14. Floor covering	29. Drainage and landscaping
15. Cabinets	

Figure 4-5: Sample Warranty Standard, Heating

Heating systems will be installed in accordance with local building codes and engineered design for each home. Adequacy of the system is determined by its ability to establish a temperature of 70 degrees, measured in the center of the room, five feet above the floor. In extremely cold temperatures (10 degrees below or colder), the system should maintain a temperature differential of 80 degrees. Thermostats are calibrated to within plus or minus 5 degrees.

Expansion or contraction of metal ductwork will typically result in some ticking or popping sounds. It is not possible to eliminate these sounds.

The heat system is not a "sealed system," but the ductwork should remain securely fastened. If it becomes unattached the Builder will repair as needed.

Heat register covers are removable & adjustable. Homeowner is responsible for adjustments to regulate the heat flow. Rooms further from the furnace will need to have vents opened more.

Placement of heat vents may vary slightly from positions in model.

An outside combustion air duct is included to supply fresh air for the furnace & water heater. The supply of fresh air is vital to the safe & efficient operation of both items & should not be limited in any way.

This sample is provided for purposes of illustration only. When developing or revising warranty documents or other legal documents, always have them reviewed by an attorney qualified for the state(s) in which they will be used.

Maintenance Guidelines

Along with the warranty standards, salespeople should be able to provide basic maintenance information. Builders often develop this information from their own knowledge and experience, often with the help of a variety of subcontractors and manufacturers (see Figures 4-6 and 4-7). Maintenance information includes descriptions of what to expect from various components of the home and what materials or steps routinely are needed in caring for the home. Builders who do not wish to write their own materials can purchase copies of booklets such as NAHB's "Your New Home and How to Take Care of It" to supply to each buyer. Either way, the information provided to the home buyer will help develop a practical sense of where warranty service ends and the customer's maintenance obligations begin.

Figure 4-6: Suggested Topics for Homeowner Maintenance Guidelines

1. Natural expansion and contraction (see Figure 4-7)
2. Heating System
3. Air conditioning
4. Humidifier
5. Plumbing
6. Electrical
7. Gas shut offs
8. Water shut offs
9. Insulation
10. Paint or stain
11. Wood trim
12. Door locks
13. Floor covering
14. Cabinets
15. Countertops
16. Fireplace
17. Concrete
18. Roof
19. Vents
20. Garage overhead door
21. Drainage and landscaping

Figure 4-7: Sample Maintenance Guideline, Natural Expansion and Contraction

All building materials are subject to expansion and contraction caused by changes in temperature and humidity. Dissimilar materials expand or contract at different rates. This results in separation between materials, particularly dissimilar ones. The effects can be seen in small cracks in drywall and in paint, especially where moldings meet sheetrock; at mitered corners, where tile grout meets tub or sink, etc. This can be alarming to an uninformed homeowner, but, in fact, it is very normal, even in the highest quality of construction. Shrinkage of the wood members of your home is inevitable. This will occur in your home. It will be most noticeable during the first year, but may continue beyond that time. In most cases, paint and caulking is all that is needed to conceal this minor evidence of a very natural phenomenon. Even properly installed caulking will shrink and must be maintained. (For additional information, refer to individual categories such as drywall, trim, tile, and countertops)

This sample is provided for purposes of illustration only. When developing or revising warranty documents or other legal documents, always have them reviewed by an attorney qualified for the state(s) in which they will be used.

Spotlighting

Any builder probably can find a topic or two that have traditionally caused problems. "Spotlighting" such trouble spots, presenting the facts and the builder's position, and obtaining the customer's initials or signature to note the review, can draw enough attention to the information to make a lasting impression on the customer. The sample handout on hardwood flooring discussed in Figure 4-8 is a typical example. Here, the information is expressed in a positive tone, without overpromising the product.

One builder has used the spotlighting technique on his pet peeve, scratches or chips in sinks and tubs. Tired of arguments from customers that they simply did not notice the damage during the walk-through, he now allows customers seven calendar days after closing to report any such damage. A one-page spotlighting handout signed at the end of the walk-through and filed with the warranty clearly describes this procedure and sets the limit. At the end of seven days, he will no longer accept any mention of this item. Customers feel this is more than fair, and the builder is not repairing or replacing any more fixtures than before. There are no longer any arguments over this subject.

Procedures

The procedures for reporting warranty items, suggested timing of those reports, how to handle emergencies (both during and after normal business hours), and what to expect in response to submitting a warranty list should all be covered the in written material the customer receives (see Figure 4-9). A sample copy of the builder's warranty service request form (or, even better, a supply—three is enough) can be included. If customers become familiar with the "put it in writing" policy early, they will find the process more comfortable if service is needed later.

Homeowner Manuals

The complete collection of materials involved in selling a home, combined with all the literature related to warranty plus, in many cases, homeowner association documents, create a very tall stack of papers. More and more builders are taking the easy and inexpensive step of organizing all of this in a logical sequence and delivering it in a notebook. The resulting "manual" can be used by the customer as a reference (see Figure 4-10). The format encourages reading, keeps all the material together, and makes a very professional impression on the buyer. The salesperson who delivers or displays the homeowner manual has a natural and comfortable way to bring up subjects such as walk-through and warranty.

Figure 4-8: Sample Spotlighting Handout

Hardwood Floors

The solid oak hardwood flooring you are about to select for your home is 100 percent natural. Although today's better finishes make caring for hardwood floors easier than ever, you should be aware of the steps required to protect and maintain the pleasing appearance. We want you to be fully informed regarding what you can and cannot expect from this product. Please consider the information below prior to making your final decision.
(The items below can be expanded upon in the handout to explain characteristics the uninformed homeowner might misinterpret as defects.)

- Because of the natural characteristics of the materials, you should not expect a tabletop finish. . . .
- The surface will not be dust free. . . .
- The floor will not be monotone . . .
- Wood floors will respond noticeably to changes in humidity level in the home, especially in the winter; a humidifier will help but will not completely eliminate this reaction.

Wood floors exhibit the following traits: When new, small splinters of wood will appear; dimples or scratches can be caused by moving furniture, dropping heavy or sharp objects, etc. Some shrinkage or warping can be expected, especially around heat vents or any heat producing appliances. Warping will occur if the floor becomes wet repeatedly or is thoroughly soaked even one time. A dulling of the finish in heavy traffic areas is likely; a white, filmy appearance is caused by moisture (often from wet shoes or boots). **Since the effects of climate, natural wear and tear, and the natural characteristics of the product cannot be prevented, our warranty does not cover these items.** Beyond any serious defects noted on the Orientation list, care of wood floors is your responsibility as a part of ongoing maintenance of the home.

The steps you can take to preserve the beauty and value of wood flooring are described on the back of this sheet. (The remainder of the handout details procedures the homeowner can follow to preserve and protect the hardwood floors. Items noted can include food spills, scuff marks, preventing damage from high heeled shoes, protective walk-off mats at the exterior doors, floor protectors on furniture, regular vacuuming and sweeping, avoidance of wet-mopping, damp-mopping with vinegar and water, not waxing a polyurethane-finished floor, and periodic recoating with polyurethane.)

Your signature below indicates your acceptance of the responsibility for care of wood floors and understanding that our warranty does not include repairs of the items listed.

_____   _____
(Buyer)   (Date)

_____   _____
(Buyer)   (Date)

Figure 4-9: Sample Handout on Procedures

Warranty Service

You will receive the signed Limited Warranty for your home at the closing. A specimen copy is provided in this manual for your review. We suggest that you carefully read through this information as well as the service procedures that are discussed below. If you have any questions regarding standards or procedures, contact either your sales representative or our warranty manager.

To comply with the terms of your warranty as well as for reasons of accuracy, all nonemergency items for which you request service must be reported in writing. "Request for Service" forms are provided for your convenience. As described below, you may also write a letter at any time. We will not accept reports of routine warranty items over the phone.

Service Checkpoints

A. Thirty-day List

In order for our service program to operate at maximum efficiency, as well as for your own convenience, we suggest that you wait 30 days prior to submitting a warranty list. This allows you sufficient time to become settled in your new home and thoroughly examine all components.

B. Eleven-month List

Near the end of the tenth month of your one year warranty, the Company will mail a reminder that the Materials and Workmanship portion of your warranty is about to expire. This will be your opportunity to check your home for items to be submitted for final warranty action. This is a service provided as a convenience to homeowners; failure to receive this notice for any reason will not constitute an extension of the warranty period.

C. Emergency Service

Emergency, as defined by the warranty, includes

1. Total loss of heat
2. Total loss of electricity
3. Plumbing leak that requires the entire water supply to be shut off
4. Total loss of hot water
5. Total sewage stoppage
6. Roof leak
7. or any situation that endangers the occupants or the home.

During business hours, call the warranty office. After hours, weekends, or holidays, call the necessary subcontractor directly. Their phone numbers are listed on the "Emergency Service" sheet you receive during your Homeowner Orientation.

D. Kitchen Appliance Warranties

The manufacturers of kitchen appliances will work directly with you if any repairs are needed for these products. Customer service phone numbers are listed in the use and care materials for the individual appliances. Be prepared to provide the model and serial number of the item and the closing date on your home. Appliance warranties are generally for one year from date of closing. Refer the literature provided by the manufacturer for complete information.

(continued on next page)

(continued from previous page)

Service Processing Procedures

A. You can help us to serve you better by including complete information.
1. Name, address, phone numbers where you can be reached during business hours
2. Community name and lot number for your home
3. A complete description of the problem. For example, "Guest bath—cold water line leaks under sink" NOT, "plumbing problem in bathroom"

B. Upon receipt of any "Service Request" letter, the warranty manager will contact you for an inspection appointment.
1. Appointments are available Monday through Friday, 8:00 am to 4:00 pm.
2. The items listed in your written request will be inspected to determine appropriate action.
3. A written service order will be issued, with a copy sent to you, notifying service personnel and authorizing repairs for your home. It is the responsibility of the service person who receives the order to contact you for an appointment. If you are difficult to reach by telephone, you are welcome to expedite this process by initiating the call to the service person.

C. Completion of service items can be expected within fifteen (15) days of the service order issue date unless you are otherwise notified.

Magnuson-Moss

To comply with the Magnuson-Moss Act (see chapter 2) a file containing copies of the manufacturers' warranty documents on consumer products should be made available for customer review in the sales office. Plastic page protectors work well to contain and protect these materials. Extra copies can be obtained easily by contacting the manufacturers directly or by using the literature from the products in a model home. Custom builders may find it useful to photocopy the warranties from consumer products and create a file of the various items installed in past homes. This requires a small extra effort when equipment is delivered to a home under construction, but it will seem worthwhile when the next customer orders the same item.

Getting the Customer to Read the Literature

"There will be a quiz later" usually fails to produce results in adults—although it may be an amusing way to begin the brief lecture that is delivered with the literature. The emphasis the salesperson puts on the literature will go a long way toward impressing customers with its importance and getting them to read it.

For additional reinforcement, sales staff members can make it a habit to ask in subsequent conversations if the customer has any questions from reading the warranty materials. When the customer comes in or calls with a question, the salesperson might

---

Figure 4-10: Information for Homeowner Manual

A great deal of information and paper is involved in selling a home. Most builders probably already have many of the items that usually go into a Homeowner Manual, although pieces may be given to the customer a little at a time. By organizing that material into a format that is logical and allows the customer to locate specific answers to questions easily, everyone involved benefits.

The objective is to make it clear what happens, when, and who has what responsibilities. The manual can address anticipated questions, identify recurring issues, and communicate clearly and honestly in a positive tone, solving problems before they come up. Answering questions before they are asked is an excellent tool to help establish correct expectations and satisfy the customer.

A Homeowner Manual can include any or all of the items listed below. The format is limited by budget and imagination. Everything from pocket folders to leather bound volumes could be used. A standard 3-ring notebook is a popular binder. This is reasonably priced and allows flexibility when changes are made.

- Helpful hints on moving
- List of items needed when applying for a mortgage
- How, when, and where the customer makes "color selections"; time frame for completing the selections
- Instructions about change orders, perhaps a sample
- Information on closing (where it takes place, how long it takes, utility service transfer and phone numbers, insurance, cash or certified funds)
- Description of the purpose and procedures for the homeowner orientation (walk-through), copy of the form used so that it will be familiar
- Homeowner maintenance information
- Customer warranty procedures and service request forms; a clear definition of "emergency" and whom to call if one occurs after hours
- Warranty standards—If an insured warranty is provided, the insurance company supplies printed standards. Builders who have created their own typically use the same measurements for defects and discuss the same topics. There is little difference in warranty standards from builder to builder; it is in interpretation, attitude, and response time that differences occur.
- Landscaping guidelines
- Homeowner Association documents, if applicable
- Community information: fire, police, hospitals, recreation, shopping, schools, government services, etc. (Libraries, chambers of commerce, and local businesses offer many free or inexpensive pieces of informative literature.)

gracefully say, "I believe that is covered in your homeowner manual; let me see if I can locate the page for you . . . Here it is, on page XX—all the phone numbers for emergency service after hours are listed. The heating contractor is . . ." and so forth. After hearing several times that the answer is in the manual, customers will see the value in reading it. Of course, for this kind of conversation to work, the salesperson must be very familiar with what is and what is *not* in the material provided. When this message is delivered the tone of voice should be cheerfully helpful; a lecturing tone may alienate the caller. Creative enticement can sometimes be well applied; for example, one builder experienced good results from delivering a gift certificate for dessert and beverage from a nearby restaurant that had a particularly wonderful reputation for their pies. The speech that accompanied the gift went along the lines of, "No one ever wants to take time to read all the 'fine print'. We feel it's so important that we're going to bribe you by paying for a slice of pie and cup of coffee. Please enjoy it while you review this information. Just get in touch with me if you have any questions at all after reading it."

Transition From Buyer to Owner

Suggesting that conducting an effective walk-through program is an important factor for the successful operation of warranty service may sound a bit strange. Upon reflection, however, it is easy to see many reasons for the relationship.

A well-planned walk-through provides the homeowner with valuable hands-on knowledge for living comfortably in the home. Who wants to have to call the warranty office to ask about setting the thermostat, turning on the self-cleaning oven, or changing the furnace filter? If the electrical circuit breaker trips, a well-informed homeowner will know what to do. Instead of reporting an outlet defective when a lamp does not come on, an informed customer will first try the wall switch. If normal effects such as "settling," cracking of concrete, fading of paint, and so on, have been read about in the builder's literature and then discussed during the walk-through, homeowners are less likely to panic when they occur.

The walk-through offers the builder one more chance to review the warranty and answer questions about standards and procedures. How to report emergency and nonemergency items, the purpose of the inspection, and the expected response time for typical service requests all can be reiterated and emphasized.

Most important of all is the service the homeowner receives in response to a warranty list. This service has a tremendous impact on the customer's attitude during the warranty period. It can literally set the tone for a year-long relationship.

Anyone can make a list on any house. Items can always be found—items of varying degrees of "nitpicky-ness." The question is, is the homeowner motivated to create the list?

Some homeowners are motivated to create lists by their nature. They have detail-oriented personalities. Other homeowners are motivated by past experiences, or by a desire or need for regular attention. Still others can be motivated by anger, frustration, and sometimes a desire to "get even" with a builder who somehow disappointed them. A homeowner who wants to make a list will be able to do so. The builder can do a lot to mitigate this desire with effective handling of the walk-through. Remembering that the warranty service will inherit the home, the customer, and the customer's opinion, service on walk-through items can make a lasting, positive contribution to that opinion.

After-Closing Contacts with Sales and Construction

No one who is concerned about customer opinion should ever utter the words, "It's not my department." This amounts to verbal shoulder shrugging. It is a real image-killer.

Equally damaging is to have a salesperson or a construction superintendent listen to a customer's warranty request, promise to pass it along to the appropriate person for action, then forget about it for three weeks. Further, when employees remark, "I don't know. Why don't you call . . . ?" it helps neither the customer nor the builder's image.

Everyone who works for a builder has two jobs. The first job is whatever is indicated on that person's business card. The second is customer service. This responsibility often translates into performing "extra" services for customers that the employees thought they had "finished" with. Every contact with anyone connected with the company contributes to the builder's or remodeler's overall image. This remains true even after the home is occupied or the work is completed and the warranty manager is technically responsible for the customer's satisfaction.

Still, employees do have routine work to do and cannot be experts in all areas of the business, including warranty. If the builder has developed an effective system for handling warranty items, it should be utilized. How can the two points of view best be reconciled?

The answer is to identify simple, effective ways for employees outside of warranty to respond when customers want to report warranty items or have questions or complaints about warranty service. In order to assist the customer without overriding the authority of warranty personnel, the best approach is to help the customer use the company's established warranty system. Keeping a supply of warranty service request forms in the sales and construction offices allows employees there to suggest that the fastest way a customer to get a defect corrected is to get it into the warranty system for attention. The employee then hands the customer the proper form, explaining that if the customer will fill it out and drop it in the mail, the warranty manager will get back in touch. Depending on geographic factors, the employee might even offer to deliver the request to the warranty office. The customer has been assisted, and the system is still being used. Construction and sales personnel have given a positive response to the customer without bypassing the system.

When the matter in question is not covered by the warranty, an effective response can be, "The person who can help us with that is Susan. Let me get her on the phone for you." This response is much different in tone from, "You'll have to call Harry about that."

If the solution is printed in the homeowner manual, the employee can assist the caller without making the homeowner feel lazy or stupid for not looking it up. For example, the employee might say, "I think there might be something about that in the manual. Let's see if we can find it; we'll both know the answer next time!"

A complaint about the service received on items that have already been reported to warranty may occasionally be heard by someone outside of the warranty office. An uninformed employee might react to such a complaint by believing that the warranty office had fallen down on the job. If the employee is familiar with how the system is intended to work, however, he or she can clarify the problem by asking a few questions. For example, the employee might ask:

- "Has the inspection been done?"
- "Did you receive a service order listing the item?"
- "Has it been longer than X days since you got the service order?"

The answers to such questions may reveal that the item was reported and service was denied. If so, the employee can refer to the written standards, suggesting, "Let's double-check the manual and see if we can find anything that might help." Seeing the written standard or maintenance information often reminds customers that they were informed about this possibility before, and some of their frustration may dissipate.

The problem may be that the homeowner has been difficult to reach for a service appointment. A response might be, "We have no problem at all with you calling the subcontractor listed on the service order to set an appointment. That is often quicker than waiting for your service order to come around on the sub's list of things to do. Let me call their number right now and see if we can get something set up."

Perhaps a subcontractor is behind schedule. The employee might say, "The warranty office monitors completion of service orders. When something is beyond its time limit, there is usually a reason. Let's call the warranty office and see if they know anything. If not, they will be most effective in solving this for you."

The customer should come away from this conversation feeling that some progress has been made, that someone on the builder's staff is genuinely interested in solving the problem. From the builder's point of view, the same goals pertain, but one more is added. The way in which a complaint is handled ideally will help the customer to understand at least one of three things:

- what the homeowner can do the next time,
- what to expect, and
- whom to contact.

All of the above examples reinforce the builder's normal warranty service system while responding to the customer in a caring manner.

Sometimes an angry customer makes a point of walking into the sales office in the middle of a busy weekend to make an interesting scene in front of several prospects—all of whom, according to the distraught salesperson, were moments from signing contracts, but ran screaming from the sales center after hearing the comments of warranty's "victim."

Sales personnel will handle these situations better if they do not appear embarrassed or humiliated. The prospects will indeed be watching closely, not because they have never heard a customer complain before, but because they are very interested in seeing how this builder handles complaints. The proper response is to make some progress in resolving the issue while staying within the system. Behaving in a way that shows a firm belief in the effectiveness and fairness of the warranty program sends a clear message to the prospects. Salespeople should be unafraid to take the time to work through the necessary questions and determine what the problem is. It is important to keep an open mind, but remain aware that the complaining customer may have a "hidden agenda."

Suppose, for example, the complaint turns out to be half a dozen minor problems in the new home, none of which have been reported to the warranty office because the homeowner does not have time to write out a list. By making a scene in the sales office, the homeowner hopes to pressure the salesperson to call in the items and get them fixed. Instead, the salesperson can simply pull out a service request and begin to fill it out. When complete, it should be given to the customer to review and sign. The salesperson then puts it into an envelope and promises to drop it into a mail box on the way home from work. A variation on this theme is to sit the customer down with a cup of coffee and the form, offering to fax it to the main office by the next business day.

Just as no one buys a home without having lived somewhere else, no one comes without having had a complaint about a product before. For the sales prospect, the interesting aspect of witnessing such a scene is observing how it is handled. When the salesperson stays calm and can think clearly, this will impress the prospect. As for the plotting customer, he or she should leave having learned that "sales office blackmail" won't work with these well-informed salespeople. If the sales team has been thoroughly instructed in the warranty system, they will know how to educate the customers and handle complaints.

5

Developing a Good Warranty Staff

Fitting Warranty Into the Organizational Chart

One person should be assigned to manage warranty. That person also may have other duties. Indeed, in smaller companies, warranty may be only one of half a dozen responsibilities handled by one individual (see Figure 5-1)—but having several people deciding warranty issues independently of each other generates a troublesome inconsistency. The only way warranty service can be managed by a group is to convene an established committee each time a warranty policy must be made or interpreted. Otherwise, the broad perspective is too easily lost and conflicting procedures or standards can quickly develop. Whether managing warranty service is a full-time assignment or a task that parallels several others, it should be assigned to one person on the staff.

Ideally, the person in charge of warranty service should report to the company's executive officer, president, or owner. Having the warranty manager report to the head of construction or sales eventually leads to internal conflicts of interest, in which warranty generally loses. The person responsible for construction or sales naturally protects that department's primary interests whenever a conflict involving warranty arises.

In smaller organizations, where warranty responsibilities *must* be assigned within either the sales or the construction department, construction is the logical choice (see Figure 5-2). A construction background is more useful than a sales background in making warranty repair judgments. Also, construction-related problems that repeatedly show up in warranty still can be identi-

Figure 5-1: Organizational Charts, One-Person and Small, Balanced Company

In a one-person company, the owner wears all the hats. One challenge is to maintain an objective balance among these varied roles, so that the builder performs well in all areas—not only those for which the person's talents or training are strongest.

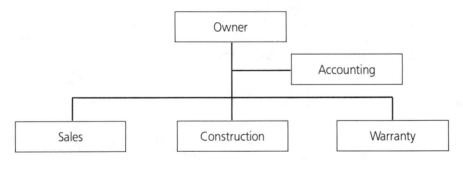

> **Owner**
>
> design
> marketing
> sales
> construction
> quality control
> walk-through
> warranty
> accounting
> other duties

As the company grows, balance must be maintained as responsibilities shift to other persons who are put in charge of major functions.

Owner — Accounting
Sales — Construction — Warranty

fied readily and corrected. Nonetheless, precedent-setting policy decisions should be reviewed or made by the owner, with careful consideration of all points of view. When only a few people are involved, quick and regular communication should be possible.

The builder has an important reason to maintain direct contact with the warranty staff. As each new service question is answered, a policy or standard is created or reinforced. Over time, these accumulated decisions create and define the builder's organization; they communicate company priorities and they express company philosophy. This process is a right and responsibility of the head policy maker.

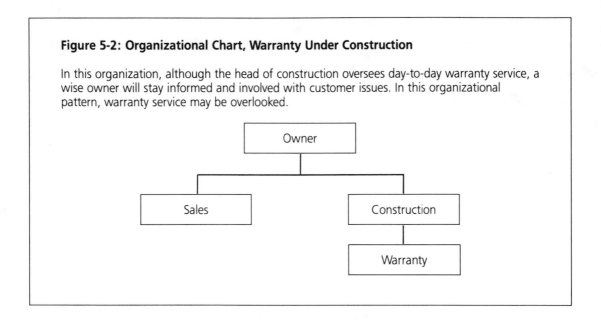

Figure 5-2: Organizational Chart, Warranty Under Construction

In this organization, although the head of construction oversees day-to-day warranty service, a wise owner will stay informed and involved with customer issues. In this organizational pattern, warranty service may be overlooked.

Manager, Director, or Vice President?

By organizing the lines of authority so that the head of warranty reports directly to the CEO, president, or owner, the voices of the sales, construction, and warranty departments are heard at equal volume. This helps create an environment in which decisions can be based on an objective view of the issue.

Larger organizations that have a vice president of construction and vice president of marketing should also have a vice president of customer relations. If company positions include a construction manager and sales manager, there should be a corresponding customer relations manager. Personal charisma and power can never be discounted, but establishing titles of equal stature allows each department's voice the opportunity to be heard.

Prepared with solid data and sound logic, an effective service professional will make the customers' viewpoint heard and respected in management meetings. The company will make better decisions if it consciously considers the impact its choices will have on service image. Just as discussing warranty service with incoming subs underscores the builder's service commitment, so creating internal authority for customer service personnel—including warranty staff—sends other managers a clear message that this matters to the builder.

In one organization that lacked this balance, the warranty manager was not included in weekly management meetings. A memo from this manager did begin an ongoing discussion about a window-caulking issue; however, the vice president of construction easily convinced the builder that the warranty division was exaggerating, and that caulking newly installed windows was unnecessary. The construction vice president argued that taking this step would increase the painter's time and the company's costs. No one from customer service was present at the management meetings to counter these arguments or present facts supporting their point of view. As a result, no change was made. The builder was not informed that three out of ten homeowners had already experienced at least one window leak and the resulting repairs already were costing the company more than the proposed caulking. No one mentioned the window manufacturer's directions, which required the caulking.

The construction division, concerned about staying on schedule, was able to use its presence at management meetings to override the warranty manager's perspective on the issue. The result was a false economy for the builder and damage to the company's image each time a new homeowner discovered the recurring defect. Furthermore, while warranty technicians spent time repairing preventable damage, normal service activities suffered significant delays.

Given an expanded view of customer service, warranty becomes just one aspect of the company's relationship with buyers. The customer service manager's responsibilities also expand. For example, the customer service manager would contribute to sales staff training and provide materials for their use in educating home buyers. Similarly, the customer service manager, together with the construction manager, can standardize procedures regarding customer site visits, the builder's homeowner orientation program, and the buyer's transition to ownership and occupancy of the home.

The customer service manager's responsibilities may involve the design, construction, and quality control functions, as well as interaction with mortgage companies, decorators, subs, closing personnel, homeowner associations, and even the company receptionist. In a larger company, this person's staff might include a warranty manager, homeowner orientation representative, in-house service technicians, and a customer relations secretary or administrator. If the builder can designate only one person to oversee the company's interactions with customers, that person should still report directly to the head policy maker (see Figure 5-3). Thus, the warranty manager continues to function in a neutral setting apart from the direct control of sales or construction.

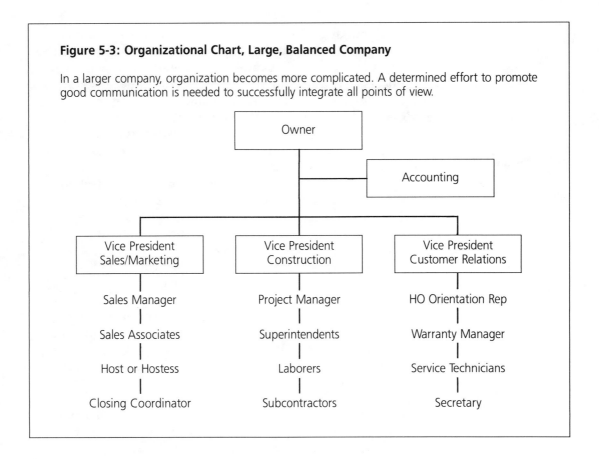

Figure 5-3: Organizational Chart, Large, Balanced Company

In a larger company, organization becomes more complicated. A determined effort to promote good communication is needed to successfully integrate all points of view.

Does a Warranty Manager Wear a Tool Belt?

Another question to consider when deciding how warranty will be handled is whether or not the warranty manager will perform repairs. For some companies, it works well to have a warranty manager carry tools and perform repairs, referring work to subcontractors only when specialized knowledge or equipment are needed. Combining inspection and repair tasks can result in one efficiently organized full-time position. This strategy can be preferable to managing numerous part-time assignments by tagging them onto the regular work of several people.

For other organizations, the desired service style dictates that the warranty manager focus on administrative tasks, conducting the inspections and issuing service orders for both in-house and subcontractor repairs. Many builders feel that the treatment homeowners receive is better when one person concentrates solely on dealing with customer questions and repair personnel are kept separate from the decision-making process.

Staffing and organizational choices also are influenced by work volume and by the skills of available personnel. Either approach can work well; the important thing is for builders to smoothly integrate customer service and warranty responsibilities within the overall company organization.

Subcontracting Warranty Service

One popular approach in recent years has been to subcontract warranty services. This strategy can benefit the smaller company that wants to provide professional level service for homeowners but cannot afford a full-time, in-house staff. When using such services, builders must check references carefully, review specific procedures and standards in detail, and maintain regular communications with the subcontractor. Builders should receive copies of all service records. Costs usually are based on a set fee per house, often a percentage of the sales price. The fee pays for the subcontractor's handling of warranty communications with homeowners, inspections, and the administration of service activities. The builder and the technical subs remain responsible for actual repair costs. Obtaining customer comments that are independent of reports from the service company can confirm whether the service company's performance supports the builder's desired reputation.

At some point, the volume and costs of service requests reach a level at which the builder considers bringing the work in-house. This process needs to be monitored carefully so that the builder's final decision is based on a complete understanding of the infrastructure needed to support current and future service.

How Many Employees Are Enough?

Builders and remodelers operate within a wide range of business environments. This range is reflected in staff size and company structure. Some builders function best with a few key people handling many responsibilities; other builders function more efficiently by creating discrete divisions, each having its own staff and hierarchy. Every company seeks that unique balance between flexibility and structure that will motivate employees to their best level of performance. When builders look at staffing needs from the standpoint of time management—how many person-hours it will take to perform specified customer-service tasks—the puzzle of integrating warranty service into an existing staff structure begins to reveal its own solutions.

Service Technicians

Calculating how many warranty technicians a builder will need means simply dividing the number of homes to be built by the number of homes one technician can care for. The difficulty comes when the builder tries to determine the number of homes one service technician can effectively cover. To arrive at this number the builder must consider several factors besides a target budget.

Geography. If the builder is active in eleven communities spread over a couple of hundred miles, the number of homes that can be serviced effectively by one person will decrease. If all the homes are within five miles of the main office, the number will increase.

Quality Control. If the builder has a strong quality control program, there will be fewer warranty items per house. The number of homes one technician can manage will therefore increase. If the technicians on the warranty staff begin to outnumber the other employees in the company, however, it may be time for the builder to increase quality control efforts.

Size and Design of Product. Smaller homes usually have fewer warranty items than larger homes, even at the same quality level. There is less opportunity for problems to occur in a 950 square-foot home than in a 3,400 square-foot home. However, size alone is not the defining factor when evaluating the type of product. A small townhome with a lot of trim and many sophisticated details can generate more warranty repairs than a large detached home that is fairly plain. Larger homes or homes with complex designs will require more time per technician to execute warranty repairs.

Division of Work. The builder must consider which repairs will be performed by staff and which by subcontractors, either as part of their warranty obligation or as a paid service. If in-house personnel normally will conduct minor drywall repairs, paint touch-up work, and the like, the number of homes each employee can effectively cover will be lower than if subcontractors routinely provide these services.

Courtesy Repairs. Courtesy repairs (items not required according to a strict interpretation of the warranty, such as touching up caulk and grout or making weatherstrip adjustments) drastically affect workload for warranty personnel. The builder's target market may dictate a particular level of service and attention, including courtesy repairs. Young families will often have very different expectations from those of retired home buyers. Generally, higher end markets require more courtesy repairs and extra services.

Competition. The builder with the best service reputation clearly has an edge over competitors. But as soon as a builder's toughest competitor announces some terrific new service feature, pressure builds to meet the challenge and maintain that edge. Of course, service innovations need not require adding staff in the warranty department. The builder must balance workload and staffing levels, however, if the company is to remain flexible in responding to innovations.

Staff Experience and Training. A well-seasoned warranty service veteran can complete more service orders faster than a rookie. The veteran probably has also developed some skill in working with customers. An experienced technician may be well worth the extra dollars, not only in terms of actual work completed but also in terms of customer good will. Again, the judicious use of subs can help round out areas where staffs lacks technical expertise.

Materials and Parts. Lack of materials can be a major obstacle to efficient repair service. If each assignment must include a trip to a hardware store, or if the approval process for large-item purchase orders causes delays, more time will be spent on each home and more people will be required to provide service.

Managing Customer Relationships. When customers are satisfied with their homes and their builder, they are less motivated to make demands. The builder who is working to improve a damaged service reputation, however, will likely receive more requests for service and will probably be under considerable pressure to be generous in responding.

Suddenly what began as a simple formula becomes quite complicated. Adjusting the estimate of staffing needs up and down to accommodate each new factor can bring the decision-making process to a halt. A way to temper this problem is to work backwards from realistic service goals. The builder can examine what is being accomplished with current staff: What is the quality of the work? How long is it taking? Is the company meeting its service goals? If the answer to this last question is no, one option is to add more people. If current goals are adequately met, the number of people on staff is probably just right. If service personnel spend a lot of idle time in the office, a cutback may be justified.

The number of service technicians required to meet company goals will change with the seasons and with fluctuations in sales activities. A slowdown in sales will not affect the warranty department until months later. The opposite usually is true also: an increase in sales will take a while to show up in the warranty workload. Checking the number of personnel needed in warranty on a regular basis helps builders make adjustments promptly to avoid either getting behind in service or wasting dollars through overstaffing.

Employees who can perform in several roles can rotate as needed among warranty, construction, or office functions. For new superintendents, a couple of months working in warranty and seeing the result of the construction effort will provide valuable insights.

Administrative Staff

The same process applies when determining administrative staff requirements. A builder's service success is just as vulnerable to a failure in administrative processing as to a failure in technical quality. If the volume of administrative work is so great that telephone messages go unreturned for more than half a day, if service orders are not issued within one day of authorization, or if records cannot be kept current, more personnel may be needed. Trying to increase output simply by increasing pressure on current staff probably will fail. Instead, the builder can track and measure the company's customer service activities, from initial contact through completion of the home and warranty service. Observation will confirm whether staff and subs are making a conscientious effort and whether training is adequate. The builder can search out and reduce or eliminate any inefficiencies. Then the builder can adjust the number of administrative employees as needed to achieve the company's stated goals.

It is usually better to increase staff efficiency and quality control efforts rather than to simply allow the warranty staff to grow and grow. Reacting to poor product quality by increasing repair capabilities treats the symptom while ignoring the cause. In the rush of sales and construction activities, at times it can seem tempting to let the warranty department compensate for problems or inefficiencies that arise in other departments. In effect, this approach makes "customer relations repair" one of the regular duties of the department. In the long run, this is an expensive option—and bad customer service. Establishing conscious, realistic goals regarding the volume of warranty repair work helps builders avoid this temptation.

Hiring Warranty Staff

Once the positions to be filled have been identified and located on the company organizational chart, the hiring search can begin. A unique combination of talents will be found in a good warranty service employee. When hiring, the builder can begin to identify those talents by considering the specific needs of each position.

A warranty manager's work demands highly developed organizational and communication skills, combined with a personality that can remain friendly and courteous while being firm and sometimes assertive (see Figure 5-4). The individual sought must remain calm and effective in emergencies, controlled under stress. A healthy ego, a good sense of humor, and the ability to take criticism without taking it personally enable an employee to last longer and perform more effectively as a warranty manager.

Figure 5-4: Sample Job Description, Warranty Manager

Position   — WARRANTY MANAGER
Department   — Warranty
Reports to   — Owner
Supervises   — Service Technician(s)
                     Warranty Secretary
                     Subcontractors

GENERAL JOB DESCRIPTION
Implement procedures to provide effective warranty service for all customers following the limited warranty and established standards and policies.

MAJOR DUTIES AND RESPONSIBILITIES
1. Inspect items reported, record observations and decisions on each service requested.
2. Initiate service for acknowledged warranty items, designating an appropriate subcontractor or in-house employee.
3. Monitor completion of assigned service work; investigate homeowner complaints and resolve discrepancies between intended service and actual work.
4. Place follow-up calls to homeowners upon completion of service orders.
5. Serve as liaison between subcontractors and homeowners.
6. Prepare and circulate monthly reports on subcontractor rate of completion of service orders.
7. Instruct subcontractors regarding specific procedures and time frames.
8. Monitor warranty items for recurring problems.
9. Assist with product improvement by investigating repeating items with construction and purchasing to eliminate them at their source.
10. Update sales and construction regarding significant changes in warranty procedures.
11. Answer warranty related questions from superintendents and homeowners.

At the same time, a thorough construction background is clearly desirable. Familiarity with construction sequence, the fundamentals of scheduling, and construction techniques and terminology all help get the job done. Appearance cannot be overlooked. Dress and grooming can be important contributors to overall company image. Finally, the person should fit comfortably into the company culture.

Hands-on warranty repair work requires technical skills and general construction knowledge (see Figure 5-5). This person must be able to perform a variety of repairs quickly and correctly while maintaining a positive relationship with the customer. A service technician who can repair any problem but who offends every homeowner is no more useful to the builder than one who gets along well with the customers but does not know how to repair anything. Diplomacy, discretion, patience, and time-management skills are all needed. Again, appearance must be considered: if homeowners are reluctant to allow a warranty technician into their homes, that person will not complete many service orders.

Anyone connected with a warranty program must be able to think through a situation objectively, sort through the factors involved (including hidden agendas), fairly determine what action should be taken, and proceed with what needs to be done.

Figure 5-5: Sample Job Description, Warranty Technician

Position   — WARRANTY TECHNICIAN
Department   — Warranty
Reports to   — Warranty Manager

GENERAL JOB DESCRIPTION
Provide services and repairs as assigned for homeowners and showhomes.

MAJOR DUTIES AND RESPONSIBILITIES
1. At all times present a positive image of the company to the customer, demonstrating courtesy and professionalism in every task and communication.
2. Contact homeowners to set service appointments, arrange for availability of needed materials and perform repairs as assigned.
3. Order supplies, parts, and materials needed to complete service orders.
4. Return completed service orders daily to warranty office, noting any items that require follow up attention and documenting any back charges.
5. Maintain assigned tools, equipment, and vehicle in good and safe condition at all times.
6. Know and follow all standards and procedures unless authorized by warranty manager to make an exception.
7. Perform assigned repairs in showhomes.

Recognizing when circumstances warrant making an exception to normal policy and knowing how to obtain the necessary authorization to proceed is vital. This ability to take initiative within the context of builder-established policies, find satisfactory responses, and set priorities is critical when homeowners or emergencies compete for attention.

In interviewing candidates for warranty positions, it can be helpful to describe an actual situation and allow the prospective employee to comment. By going through this exercise, the builder will get an idea of the prospect's expertise and attitude. This technique is not intended to elicit right or wrong answers; the object of the activity is to determine whether the philosophies of the builder and the candidate are compatible.

If a person with the exact combination of desired traits cannot be found, it makes sense to look for someone with people skills and add construction training. With planned field experience a bright, motivated individual will learn this quickly.

When the builder has found someone with the right mix of people skills and construction background, a thorough orientation is in order. This can begin with a review of all warranty-related documents: The purchase and sale agreement, warranty, standards, maintenance information, policies, procedures, and all forms and reports. The new employee should visit all sales offices and model centers. Tours of homes at various stages of construction should be planned so that construction sequence and specific builder techniques can be observed. This provides an opportunity for new warranty employees to meet subs and establish lines of communication.

Ongoing Development

Enrichment of construction knowledge should be part of every builder's training program. Understanding how a house is built is fundamental to making good warranty decisions and explaining them to homeowners. This knowledge can be increased through short meetings with engineers, subcontractors, manufacturer's reps, and other experts.

Arranging regular meeting times between warranty, sales, and construction departments will keep all staff updated on changes and help dissipate the friction that develops when one group does not understand why another operates a certain way. Good, regular communication is critical to effective daily functioning of the three departments, even if each department consists of only one or two people.

A regular reporting format and timetable helps connect warranty to management. Feedback should monitor the service activity itself and call attention to items that might need to be changed in the sales presentation or construction process.

A quarterly review of warranty-related expenses and projections for the budget is adequate and appropriate. The warranty staff needs to be aware of expenditures even though they cannot reasonably make decisions about legitimate repairs based only on budgetary goals. This aspect of the business might, however, influence policy or decisions on courtesy repairs. All personnel should be reminded of the need to spend company dollars wisely. One way to help employees stay more aware of costs is to inform them about the financial impact of their activities.

Field tours that include seeing competitors' products should occur a minimum of twice a year. Field tours help warranty personnel keep abreast of current practices. As a further benefit, seeing the competition provides a more balanced perspective on the company's own efforts. Hearing complaints all day every day about the defects in their company's homes, warranty employees can become convinced their product is not up to par. Regular comparison with competitors' products will effectively counter this tendency.

A customer service library that includes books, periodicals, and tapes is easy to establish. Such a library quickly grows into a valuable resource for specific ideas and general attitude adjustment, providing current material on issues such as stress management, time management, negotiation, and supervision.

Seminars also provide a fast and reasonably priced way to upgrade or refresh employees' skills and understanding. Even a veteran can benefit from a day away from the normal routine to think about how things are done and where the department's activities might be polished a bit. Some builders offer their employees partial reimbursement for the costs of work-related seminars; others pay such costs outright. Some builders do not assume the costs for such programs, but find other ways to recognize the initiative of employees who attend professional training or development programs.

Compensation

On the surface, warranty service activities appear to cost the builder considerable dollars while producing no income. Because warranty's relation to income is indirect, builders sometimes are reluctant to pay top salaries to warranty staff. If the builder keeps in mind that warranty service is an essential contributor to the company's reputation and future business, this perspective changes. Warranty expenses then are seen as a part of the company's overall marketing investment.

For years, builders have heard that the cost to draw a prospect into a builder's sales office ranges from $200 to $600 per person—with no guarantee of results. A poor service reputation repels prospects and can be the deciding factor between two builders if a buyer feels all other factors are equal. Increasing advertising expenditures to compensate for a poor service reputation is an inefficient way to spend hard-earned profits. Providing quick, effective warranty repairs are a legal obligation that must be performed in any event. By adding a little enthusiasm, by performing this obligatory service *well*, the builder also can generate the most powerful form of advertising available, the recommendations of satisfied customers.

Given this view, scrimping on salaries for warranty personnel makes little long-term sense. Finding the right people in the first place is difficult and often time consuming. Orientation and ongoing training costs add to the investment. Losing good employees wastes all that effort and can set the builder's service program back by months, perhaps even years.

The warranty manager's salary should be established at a level comparable to that of a project manager. If project managers are not included in the organization, the salary range should be slightly above the level of a superintendent. Variations in salary also will depend on the candidate's experience, on builder volume, and on the economic climate of the area. (In a larger organization where a customer relations post has been created, salaries can be much higher.) A vehicle or a travel allowance based on mileage also are often provided.

Good warranty technicians should earn an hourly wage comparable to the highest paid "hardware" people. Small hand tools are usually the employee's responsibility, with company-supplied power tools or rental equipment available when needed. Again, a vehicle may be provided or a travel allowance established based on mileage.

A dedicated warranty technician often may work more than forty hours a week. Although authorizing extra hours does not make sense when the pattern continues month after month, paying the higher rate for overtime work often is an acceptable alternative for a builder with a temporary push on service. Warranty staff usually are the kind of people who will work extra hours in a pinch to meet a challenge, but expecting them to continue at such a level over the long term is foolish for both the builder and the employees. Burnout will result eventually and the entire system will disintegrate under ceaseless pressure to accommodate more work with fewer people. Rush periods should be temporary and balanced by periods of normal workload. Additionally, smart builders will remember to recognize and appreciate staff not only for exceptional efforts but also when they maintain a high level of quality and professionalism in their routine work. Because warranty service work is essentially a team enterprise, a careful builder takes care not to accidentally undermine morale by consistently applauding one or two "stars" while overlooking the efforts of the people behind the scenes.

Before closing on the company's first home, a builder should have developed a plan for handling warranty service. This plan must include identifying who in the organization is best suited to overseeing warranty work and how that individual will be supported both in the office and in the field. A commitment to thorough orientation and ongoing training helps ensure that warranty service will keep pace with company growth.

ADMINISTERING WARRANTY SERVICE

When a house closes, copies of the color selection sheet and walk-through list are forwarded to the warranty desk. This triggers creation of the warranty file. A label is typed containing the customer's name, address, closing date, job number, and, if appropriate, a notation of the model (see Figure 6-1). Colored file labels can be used to identify the community where the home is located. The new file with its two sheets of paper is placed in the file drawer. Now what?

Figure 6-1: Warranty File Label

Jones, Tom and Mary	1/15/9X
1234 New House Street	
Job 1764	Westin-4BR

Warranty Service Structure

Typically, the kinds of promises builders make to customers involve such things as delivery date, condition of the home at delivery, warranty standards, timeliness of attention, and quality of repair work. In return for these commitments, customers make their own commitment—a financial one.

Few builders are pleased if a customer shows up for closing with $3,000 less than the agreed-upon price. Customers become just as upset when builders provide less service than they have promised. A well-thought-out warranty system combined with a well-trained staff enables the builder to make good on all commitments made during the sale.

Routine Items

Customers usually are not surprised to notice a problem or two in a new home. When something does go wrong, especially in the beginning, customers watch closely to see how it is handled. Up until this point, the builder has made promises about warranty service; now the customer will see how the builder keeps those promises. If earlier promises were kept, the customer will be optimistic. If past performance has included misunderstandings with salespeople about change orders or late delivery of the home, or if there was a long walk-through list and walk-through items were repaired grudgingly or poorly, the customer will be suspicious and worried.

According to an old Irish proverb, "if you have a reputation as an early riser, you can sleep until noon." Once the customer concludes the builder honors commitments, the customer will expect the good work to continue and will even forgive a mistake or two. On the other hand, if a customer concludes that the company operates like a slapstick comedy, it will be nearly impossible to change the person's mind.

Planning so that warranty items are handled quickly and smoothly is one secret to maintaining the desired customer opinion and keeping costs under control. Builders with haphazard warranty service often end up giving away extras in an effort to recapture lost good will. Not only is this very expensive, but the cost frequently fails to produce the intended effect. Planning begins by deciding on a structure for warranty contact. The structure will determine when and how often homeowners should report nonemergency warranty items.

Some possible approaches are shown in Figure 6-2. What appears at first to be a simple planning decision quickly becomes more complicated. Builders want to balance the schedule between too much contact and not enough; they want the walk-through items to have been completed before the first warranty list arrives; they want sufficient contact to keep customers satisfied, but not so much that a customer gets annoyed by constant traffic in and out of the home. Most important, builders will want to commit to a level of attention that they actually can provide. It is far better to promise a bit less and do it well than to promise a lot but deliver only half of it. Warranty service is

---

Figure 6-2: Choices for Customer Contact

_____ Daily

_____ Weekly

_____ Monthly

_____ Quarterly

_____ At 30 days and 11 months

_____ At 60 days and 12 months

_____ At 30 days, 6 months, and 12 months

_____ At 45 days and whenever the customer feels like it

_____ Whenever the customer feels like it (random)

_____ Whenever the builder feels like it (random)

_____ Other_____

---

not a word game. The home and the service are tangible commodities, right out in the open for the customer to see and evaluate. There is no place to hide.

By failing to set a schedule for warranty contacts, the builder selects "random" contact; any time the customer feels like sending in a list, he or she will do so. This may work out fine if the builder builds just one home a year, remodels just one kitchen, or finishes only one basement. With multiple projects, however, such a system can become chaotic. Imagine what could happen if a "random contact" is combined with a nervous homeowner:

"Mrs. Jones, I'm here to inspect the three items you reported on your May 3 warranty list."

"Great. What about the two items on my May 7 list?"

"Well, ma'am, I can't check those because today is May 8 and we don't have your May 7 list yet."

"But the work on my May 1 list isn't done and some of the same people are needed. Why can't you just add the new items to the old work orders?"

"I don't even know about them yet."

"Never mind. What happened to my April 27 list? Those two items are not done yet either."

"I really regret hearing that. We try to be quick on these things. What were the items?"

"I don't know. I've lost my April file. But I'm sure nothing's been done. I'm here all the time, you know."

"Yes, ma'am, we suspected that."

The other extreme can be equally unsatisfying. Consider suggesting that a customer save up the repair items to send them all in on one list at the end of the year:

"Mr. Jones, you have thirty minutes left on your warranty. It's time to do your year-end inspection. Where would you like to start?"

"Well, the living room is the only room left. The bedrooms fell off in the second week and the kitchen disappeared in the sixth month. Of course, the stove is still here; that 220 cord is pretty strong. The bathroom sink was missing at our orientation. The superintendent told us there was no need to write it down, though. He said he already knew about it. He never did bring it like he promised."

"I'll be . . . Mr. Jones, why didn't you call us?"

"Well, that nice salesperson of yours made such a point of explaining that your warranty service is more efficient if each homeowner just sends in one list at the end of the year, we didn't want to upset anyone."

These scenes are, of course, exaggerated. The point is that structuring customer contact allows the builder a certain amount of control. A builder can approximate what the workload will be for the warranty staff based on the history of closings. And homeowners feel more comfortable because a structure reassures them that they are in the hands of a competent professional.

The First List
Contact with the customer shortly after move-in makes sense because items that may have been missed in a walk-through inspection are likely to show up fairly quickly once the home is occupied. The builder's reputation does not benefit by allowing such items to go uncorrected for six months to a year. This is like allowing customers to walk around with a stones in their shoes. Every time someone says, "Hey, how's that new home?" the customer's answer will be, "Fine, but . . . ." Early service gets rid of the stones. Thirty, forty-five, or sixty days after move-in are common time frames for attending to first-list items.

A short letter from the warranty office reminding customers to send in this first report helps ensure a smooth transition. The letter welcomes the homeowner and acknowledges the beginning of the warranty (see Figure 6-3). Everyone likes to be noticed and appreciated. Receiving continued attention from the builder eases the feeling new homeowners sometimes get that the builder is no longer interested in their home.

Figure 6-3: Sample Welcome to Warranty Letter
(Mailed two weeks after closing.)

(Builder's Logo)

(Date)

(Customer Name)
(Address)

Dear (Customer):

   On behalf of (Builder's Company Name) I would like to welcome you to the (Community Name) community once again. We all hope that you are settled and enjoying your new home.

   While we feel that we delivered an excellent home to you, we are realistic enough to recognize that mistakes do happen. Our limited warranty spells out the services we provide in this regard.

   If you have any warranty items that need attention at this time, please complete and return the enclosed service request in the envelope provided. You may also note any items from your preclosing inspection that have not been completed or any questions you have that I might assist in answering.

   Upon receiving a service request from you, I will contact you for an inspection appointment.

   Please feel free to call me if you have any questions.

Sincerely yours,

(Signature)
Warranty Manager

Enclosures

   A follow-up customer courtesy call is a personal way to initiate contact, and carries many benefits (see Figure 6-4). It represents a level of control that satisfies the customer while giving the builder a scheduling advantage.

   Instead of waiting for a list to arrive in the mail, the builder arranges a follow-up appointment for four to six weeks after the date of closing. This is a more personal approach than the welcome-to-warranty letter, providing an even smoother transition

Figure 6-4: Sample Customer Courtesy Call
(Description provided with handouts or in Homeowner's Manual.)

The New Home
Customer Courtesy Call
. . . ensures your satisfaction with your new home.

Our Customer Courtesy Call has been created to serve three purposes: *First*, as an effective follow though to confirm that the items noted for attention during your Homeowner Orientation have been resolved; *second*, as a convenient method for you to report any new items that may need attention, items that can be overlooked until you are actually living in your new home; and *third*, as an opportunity for you to review any of the topics we discuss/demonstrate during the Homeowner Orientation. During that important meeting you may have a great many things on your mind and consequently we are prepared to review these topics if you wish.

A Simple, Convenient Procedure.

During the Homeowner Orientation you will be given several "Warranty Service Request" sheets. We ask that you use one of these to make note of any item or question you wish to bring to our attention—things you think of or notice during the first few weeks in your new home.

Approximately three weeks after your settlement date, our warranty office will contact you to arrange an appointment for your Customer Courtesy Call. This is usually scheduled for thirty days after settlement.

Customer Courtesy Call appointments are available Monday through Friday, 8:00 a.m. to 4:00 p.m. Our representative will come to your home to visit with you regarding the three areas listed above—Orientation list items, new warranty items, and any questions.

If it is more convenient, you are welcome to mail your written list to our warranty office at a later date.

Following the Customer Courtesy Call, future warranty claims can be submitted by completing a "Warranty Service Request" or simply by writing a letter. In an emergency, always feel free to call us immediately.

We appreciate your business long after the sale and we want you to know it!

from buyer to owner. Another option is to combine the two approaches, with some editing of the letter. No customer is left out; builders should not assume that homeowners are satisfied just because no one hears from them.

The customer will have heard about the warranty program during the sales process and again at the walk-through. The follow-up appointment can even be scheduled at the end of the walk-through. Knowing that this meeting is planned, the homeowner is less likely to call with questions or send in a premature list. The builder appears well organized and the customer's comfort level soars. Someone is in charge and planning to take care of things; the customer can relax. The motivation to make a warranty list dwindles in this high-trust atmosphere. Many customers feel so good about their new home they gladly take care of minor items themselves.

When service on walk-through items will be confirmed in a follow-up visit, superintendents tend to be more meticulous in confirming proper completion of the original list. This further reinforces the customer's trust. The tone of the entire process of moving and settling improves.

For a builder unused to this system, the first step to implementing such a procedure can be sending the welcome-to-warranty letter. Several months later, as workload comes under control, telephone contact can be added as a follow-up to the letter. Describing the customer courtesy call is then added to the items covered in the sales presentation and the walk-through agenda. Finally, the structure is fully applied by warranty staff. This system involves minimal extra work for the builder; an inspection visit would be scheduled to cover the customer's warranty list when it was sent in anyway. Using this system, the courtesy call serves additional purposes and can drastically reduce transition problems.

The Six-month Mistake

A few builders have tried a thirty-day, six-month, and eleven-month inspection schedule. Too often, these builders find the items from the first list still unresolved at the six-month inspection. This can result when the builder lacks adequate staff to keep up with this level of attention or when scheduling subcontractors is a problem. The builder's warranty staff suffers serious frustration. They feel as if they are entangled repeatedly in the same houses, with the same homeowners, and over the same issues. A great deal of staff time will be spent answering telephone calls from customers who want to know why service has not been completed, when the next inspection will be scheduled, and why service orders have not been sent out.

If effective service is provided on the first list, the homeowner will be reassured and less likely to make random calls. Understanding that serious items can be turned in at any time, the customer will accept the builder's suggestion that for the convenience of all concerned, the next expected contact will be near the end of the warranty.

Year-end Contact

By year-end, the home has been thoroughly tested and some minor items may require attention. The homeowner usually has recovered from the trauma of closing and moving, and no longer needs such close attention. A letter advising the customer that the warranty is nearing expiration often is sufficient (see Figure 6-5). The fact that the builder has invited a final list demonstrates the company's interest in ongoing satisfaction and adds a professional touch to the service program. This step can also prevent arguments about a list that is submitted late (outside even the thirty-day "grace" period provided by most warranties). The experience of many builders has shown that sending such a letter does not increase the number of lists submitted to the builder. Again, the letter establishes an atmosphere of concern, willingness to serve, and customer appreciation. Even if the builder's

---

Figure 6-5: Sample Year-end Letter

(Builder's Logo)

(Date)
(Customer Name)
(Address)

Dear (Customer):

It has been over ten months since you settled on your new (Builder's Company Name) home. We hope you have found your home and the surrounding community to be a pleasant and comfortable place to live.

As you are aware, the Materials and Workmanship portion of your (Builder's Company Name) warranty will expire on (Date).

If there are any items in your home that require warranty attention, please fill out the enclosed Service Request and return it in the envelope provided to our office by (Date).

Upon receipt of your report we will contact you for an inspection of the items, schedule needed repairs, and answer any questions that you may have.

Sincerely yours,

(Signature)
Warranty Manager

Enclosure

letter goes unanswered, its receipt will make a positive impression on the homeowner.

Emergency Items

Reports of emergency items should be accepted by telephone and responded to immediately, on the same day if possible. What constitutes an *emergency* should be defined clearly for the customer, and dependable emergency procedures fully explained (see Figure 6-6). Complete agreement by the subs is also essential. Although emergency procedures should seldom be needed, if they are not in place serious consequences can evolve.

Occasionally a customer will decide that a nonemergency item is an emergency and demand emergency-level service—lack of air conditioning is the classic example. In such cases, the builder will consider the character of the customer, the circumstances, and the nature of the request, then make the necessary judgment call. This requires balancing respect for the customer's feelings against the impact that setting a precedent may have on this customer and the customer's neighbors. Including the phrase, "or any item that endangers the occupants" in the definition of *emergency* allows the builder to designate as an emergency an item not otherwise listed in the definition; it also invites the homeowner to do the same.

Information-Only Items

No matter how much documentation the builder provides, sooner or later a customer will need some bit of information that was not included with the warranty. Customers also often

---

Figure 6-6: Sample Statement Defining Emergency

An emergency, as defined by the warranty, must involve

- Total loss of heat
- Total loss of electricity
- Plumbing leakage that requires the entire water supply to be shut off
- Total loss of water
- Total sewer stoppage
- or any situation that endangers the occupants of the home.

This sample is provided for purposes of illustration only. When developing or revising warranty documents or other legal documents, always have them reviewed by an attorney qualified for the state(s) in which they will be used.

request information or documents they have lost or misplaced. Although providing a well-organized homeowner manual reduces the number of these requests, a few still will be received. A friendly attitude in assisting here is as significant to a good service image as any other work done by warranty personnel. Looking up cabinet style names, paint color numbers, and similar information can take up a lot of time. Filing the buyer selection sheet with the warranty will make such tasks much easier.

Having this information readily available is not just a courtesy to the customer. It also provides the warranty office with complete details for service orders. It is very difficult to get the cabinet company to replace a kitchen drawer if the color and style are not noted on the service order. Attention to these details often makes the difference in providing excellent service. Subcontractors appreciate not having to track down the information themselves. When needed details are missing, the service order may, conversely, fall to the bottom of the sub's priorities. (Along these same lines, having a master set of prints showing cabinet layouts, window sizes, and other details on hand in the warranty office makes issuing and completing service orders proceed much faster.)

Master Warranty Calendar

To keep all the activities firmly in mind, a one-page overview of warranty service functions can be helpful (see Figure 6-7). The structure of customer contact and all follow-up activities can be reduced to brief phrases. This master calendar allows builders to analyze workload, adjust staffing needs, recognize printed material requirements, and—most importantly—discover weak spots. The follow-up and reporting activities are the items most often overlooked.

The overall operation of the warranty office should serve two general functions. The first is to correct a homeowner's immediate problem; the second is to help the builder improve the company's product. A well-run warranty office is instrumental in channeling information about recurring problems back into the organization so their causes can be eliminated (see chapter 9).

Marketing Through Warranty

The warranty process offers natural opportunities for continued customer contact and referrals. A preaddressed postcard included with service orders can be printed with builder announcements on half of one side, and a standard request for customer com-

Figure 6-7: Sample Service Calendar

Master Service Calendar

Daily	Weekly	Monthly	Quarterly	Annually
Answer phone	Staff meeting	Welcome letters	Warranty budget review	Revise Homeowner Manual
Issue service orders	Sales Office visit	Update control sheets	Performance reviews	Prepare budget
Pull completed orders	Prepare new files	Year-end letters	New sub orientation meetings	
Filing	Call subs re: old service	Update exposure chart	Thank-you letters to subs	
Type Homeowner letters	Homeowner calls re: old service orders	Pull expired files	Homeowner maintenance newsletter	
Leap tall buildings		Sub report		

ments on the back. Marketing contacts can be readily scheduled to coordinate with warranty service contacts. Customer surveys, greeting cards (such as one last "thank you for your business" on the anniversary of the closing), quarterly newsletters, updates on seasonal maintenance tasks, and announcements of close-outs, new designs, or grand openings all can be coordinated with the master warranty calendar. Direct mail marketing lists, surveys, and special public relations activities should continue to include veteran customers long after their warranties have expired.

Processing Warranty Requests

However the builder organizes warranty contacts, the next challenge is to organize the processing of the individual items reported. There are four steps to be considered: input, analysis, response, and follow-up (see Figure 6-8). Each step has its own purpose and pitfalls.

Input

Requirements for written reports are much easier for customers to accept if the builder provides a *service request* form. Two

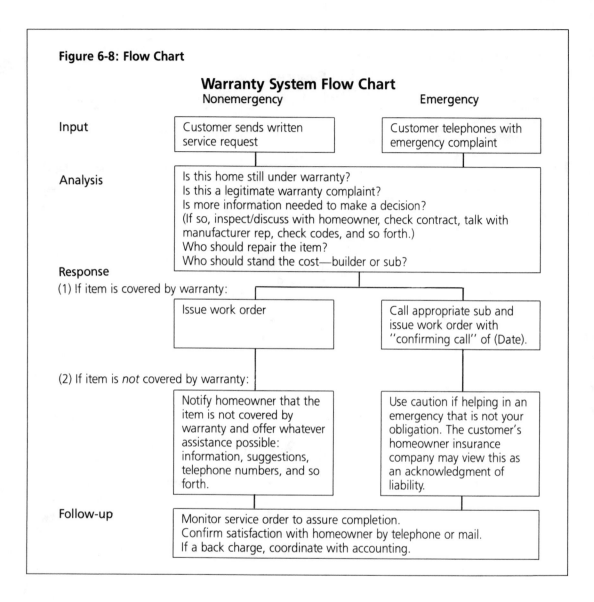

Figure 6-8: Flow Chart

Warranty System Flow Chart

	Nonemergency	Emergency
Input	Customer sends written service request	Customer telephones with emergency complaint
Analysis	Is this home still under warranty? Is this a legitimate warranty complaint? Is more information needed to make a decision? (If so, inspect/discuss with homeowner, check contract, talk with manufacturer rep, check codes, and so forth.) Who should repair the item? Who should stand the cost—builder or sub?	
Response (1) If item is covered by warranty:	Issue work order	Call appropriate sub and issue work order with "confirming call" of (Date).
(2) If item is *not* covered by warranty:	Notify homeowner that the item is not covered by warranty and offer whatever assistance possible: information, suggestions, telephone numbers, and so forth.	Use caution if helping in an emergency that is not your obligation. The customer's homeowner insurance company may view this as an acknowledgment of liability.
Follow-up	Monitor service order to assure completion. Confirm satisfaction with homeowner by telephone or mail. If a back charge, coordinate with accounting.	

types of this form are common. The first and best known is the multiple-item service request form (Figure 6-9). The date the form is received should be noted or stamped at the top, and the written request is stapled to an inspection sheet (Figure 6-10) and entered on a service request log (Figure 6-11). The homeowner is then contacted to schedule an inspection appointment.

A second choice is a single-item service request form (Figure 6-12). This form typically is provided on three-part NCR paper. The homeowner retains one copy and mails the other two to the builder. A separate form is completed for each item. Again, the

Figure 6-9: Sample Service Request Form
(Sometimes on two- or three-part NCR paper, sometimes on company letterhead.)

Warranty Service Request

With the exception of specified emergencies, all requests for service must be in writing. This provides permanent documentation for your file.

Please use this form to notify us of warranty items. Mail it the address shown above. We will contact you to set an inspection appointment. Service orders will be issued for work to be performed. Appointments for inspection or service work can be made from 8:00 a.m. to 4:00 p.m., Monday through Friday.

Name_____ Date_____

Address_____ Community_____

Phone/Home_____ Lot_____

Work_____ Plan_____

Work_____ CLOSING DATE_____

SERVICE REQUESTED

SERVICE ACTION

Comments:_____

Homeowner

date received should be noted, the request(s) logged, and an inspection appointment arranged. (This form can serve three purposes: requesting service, guiding the inspection, and recording the service order.)

Figure 6-10: Sample Inspection Sheet

Warranty Inspection

Community _____   Day _____

Lot # _____   Date _____

Plan _____   Time _____

Closing _____   By _____

Homeowner _____

Address _____

Telephone (h) _____ _____   (w) _____

                                            (w) _____

Notes   **Action**

_____   _____

_____   _____

_____   _____

_____   _____

_____   _____

_____   _____

_____   _____

_____   _____

_____   _____

_____   _____

_____   _____

_____   _____

_____   _____

_____   _____

Figure 6-11: Sample Service Request Log

Warranty Service Request Log

Date	Customer Lot #	# Items	Action: Inspect, work orders, denial letter, responsible party.

Reports of emergency items that are taken over the telephone are best recorded on a standard *warranty request form* or a file report form (see Figure 6-13). The file report form calls immediate attention to the fact that the information it contains was taken over the telephone. That may not be evident if the normal service request form is used. Either way, a copy of the record should be mailed to the customer. Maintaining a complete and accurate warranty file in the builder's office provides valuable protection to the customer. By following up with a copy for the customer, the builder demonstrates exceptional thoroughness and integrity.

During busy times, a builder may be a bit slower in contacting homeowners for their nonemergency inspection appointments. Just letting the customer know the request has been received by

Figure 6-12: Single-item Service Request Form
(Three-part form.)

Warranty Service Request

With the exception of specified emergencies, all requests for service must be in writing. Please use this form to notify us of a warranty item. Use a separate form for each item you report. The white copy provides documentation for your file. Mail the blue and yellow copies to the Company. We will contact you to set an inspection appointment. When approved the blue copy will become the service order sent to the subcontractor. Appointments for inspection or service work can be made from 8:00 a.m. to 4:00 p.m. Monday through Friday.

Name_____   Date_____

Address_____   Community_____

Phone/Home_____   Lot_____

      Work_____   Plan_____

      Work_____   Closing Date_____

Service Requested:_____

_____

_____

Office Use:

Service Request #_____   Inspection required_____

Appointment_____   Inspected by_____

Service Authorized:_____

_____

_____

Service to be provided by   _____

                             _____

                             _____

                             _____

                             _____

                             _____

Service order issue date: _____

Expected completion date: _____

_____   _____
Completion date   Service Technician

Subcontractor: Upon completion, sign and date this service order and return it to the main office. Thank you for your assistance.

mailing out a postcard (Figure 6-14) the same day can relieve some of the pressure (and telephone calls) that can result from a seasonal overload.

The telephone is here to stay, so builders may as well make peace with the thing. Try as they might, there will always be a homeowner who insists on reporting nonemergency items over the telephone. A wise builder will not allow such a minor point to become a major argument. After reviewing the normal pol-

Figure 6-13: Sample File Report

Warranty File Report

Name_____   Date_____

Address_____   Community_____

Phone/Home_____   Lot_____

    Work_____   Plan_____

    Work_____   Closing Date_____

Date/Message or Item   Action/response

_____   _____

_____   _____

_____   _____

_____   _____

_____   _____

_____   _____

_____   _____

_____   _____

Follow-up Notes

_____

_____

_____

by_____

Figure 6-14: Sample Postcard Acknowledgment

Date _____

Dear _____ ,

This is to acknowledge that your warranty service request dated _____
has been received by our office and

☐ the item(s) listed is/are covered by the warranty. Service orders will be issued within the
next five days.

☐ we will be contacting you during the next several days to make an appointment to inspect
the items listed.

☐ the items listed are subject to direct action by the appliance manufacturer. Please contact
_____ at _____ to schedule a service appointment.

☐ _____
_____

Please call me if you need other information, at (_____)_____-_____. I will be happy to
answer any questions you might have.

_____
Warranty Representative

icy—and the reasons for it—the builder can record the items dictated over the telephone. The items can be noted on the usual form, and this service request then mailed to the customer for review and approval as to accuracy. The customer then signs and mails it back to the builder for processing.

All written warranty requests should be entered on a *service request log* (Figure 6-12). This log simplifies tracing the receipt and disposition of a service request. When Ms. Jones calls on Wednesday to ask, "Did you get the list I sent last Friday?" anyone can check the log and determine whether it arrived and if it was assigned for inspection. Ms. Jones can be assured that she will be contacted shortly for an inspection appointment.

Another use of the log is to track the number of requests received in a given time period and to develop a historical record of seasonal workload. This information can be useful in anticipating staffing needs. A sudden increase in service requests from one community may call attention to developing quality problems or a salesperson who is overzealous in making promises.

The entries take just a few minutes; the information can save hours. (An ordinary steno pad can work as well as a printed sheet.)

Builders usually prefer not to accept reports on a property from a nonowner (for example a real estate agent or a hired inspector). Under the terms of the warranty, the builder has the right to refuse to act on such reports. Exceptions can be made for special circumstances if the builder's judgment indicates that would be wise. For their own protection, builders might request written notification from the homeowner that the communication has been authorized and that permission to enter the home is given. Authorized by the homeowner and accepted by the builder, such requests are processed according to the same procedures and standards as any other warranty request. (Builders should not have a second set of standards for real estate agents and inspectors.)

The temptation may be strong to give the homeowners lists of telephone numbers and instructions to call subs directly, involving the builder only if a problem develops. Generally, however, builders should resist this urge unless all the subs have an outstanding performance record and unquestionable integrity. The builder's interest in maintaining a high-quality product demands he be kept aware of the number and type of warranty items being repaired. A homeowner's problems with a sub can permanently damage the relationship with the builder. One notable exception to this is national appliance manufacturers. They have a proven track record and need not be monitored as closely as small local tradespeople.

Analysis

Analysis involves deciding whether the defect should be fixed and, if so, who should do the fixing. In analyzing warranty service requests, the logical first question is whether the home is still covered under warranty. Even if a written warranty has expired, implied warranties may come into play; the expiration of an express warranty does not always free the builder from any obligation. Nonetheless, applicability of coverage always should be part of the builder's thinking. Perhaps the items were reported during warranty but not corrected; or, the defects may be of a type that the builder will correct even if the warranty has expired. (For instance, one homeowner contacted a builder to say he had been in the attic over his family room for the first time in the three years he had lived in his home. To his surprise, he discovered that there was no insulation. The builder immediately called the insulation company and they sheepishly took care of it within the week.) Any deviation from applicable building codes would normally be corrected.

Figure 6-15 lists some sources of information that builders may call upon to arrive at a fair decision. Warranty managers need not make decisions in a vacuum. Uncertainty usually indicates a need for more information. The important point is to be certain that all the facts are considered objectively in arriving at an answer for the customer.

Inspections. Most of the time, a visual inspection will be all that is needed to determine the cause of the problem, its legitimacy under the warranty, and who should be sent to repair it. Occasionally, it may be necessary to collect additional information in order to make appropriate decisions.

Arriving on time for an inspection appointment gets the meeting off to a positive start. If the warranty rep is meeting the

---

Figure 6-15: Checklist of Information Sources

The following items should be available for consultation when questions arise:
_____ Individual customer files
_____ Contract and color selection sheet/options/change orders
_____ Quality control inspections
_____ Walk-through list
_____ Warranty requests and letters
_____ Telephone logs
_____ Correspondence from the customer; previous letters to the customer
_____ Photographs or diagrams
_____ Control sheets
_____ Building code manual

Telephone numbers for the following key contact people should be kept current and readily available:
_____ Purchasing manager for product specs
_____ Construction personnel
_____ Sales staff for information on contracts, change orders, and so forth
_____ Subcontractors
_____ Building Department inspectors
_____ Manufacturer representatives
_____ Engineer
_____ Builder's Lawyer or company lawyer

homeowner for the first time, it is appropriate to make the normal introductions, shake hands, and offer a business card. Items reported should be viewed in as logical an order as possible to save time. As each item is inspected, the warranty rep should provide an answer as to what action is provided for under the warranty. If an item is not covered, some information can be offered on what the homeowner can do to resolve the problem. Each item reviewed should be checked off and appropriate notes made on the inspection sheet (or single-item service request form) indicating the decision on that item. Photographs (especially useful with drainage problems), diagrams, and direct quotes from the customer also can be added to the inspection notes. Follow-up questions should be written down.

The warranty rep should allow sufficient time to review and discuss each item, particularly if the homeowner has submitted a detailed list of minor items. Hurrying while trying to convince a customer that the service requested is inappropriate can create resentment. Taking a few extra minutes during the inspection to explain warranty decisions can prevent hours of arguing later. Above all else, an objective attitude is required. Warranty decisions should not be made based on the personality of the customer, or on the personal feelings (good or bad) of the inspector. Facts and physical evidence should be considered and a decision made based on a fair interpretation of the standards.

Unusual Situations.

The builder's warranty standards should be clear and reasonable. Standards should be interpreted and applied consistently and fairly. Unfortunately, even these practices do not guarantee easy decisions.

Perhaps one of the toughest "gray areas" in warranty service is the defect that is so marginal it is difficult to see. These are always the repairs that cost a lot to execute—and what is worse, they always seem to be the defects that particularly annoy the homeowner. For example, a drywall defect reported by a customer could not be seen during the inspection. The defect was visible only at night when the reading lamp was on. A well-written homeowner manual would have stated that flaws in drywall that are visible only under certain lighting conditions would not be repaired. Experiences such as this suggest new items for the builder's standards and manual.

Service may be denied when the requested repair, if provided, carries a serious potential of creating a worse situation than the original problem. Drywall again offers a good example: a minor texture flaw can become a major eyesore if touched up, particularly on an enameled wall. Acknowledging that the flaw exists but counseling the homeowner that the repair may make it worse will convince most people to accept a minor defect as part of the personality of the home.

Sometimes it helps to ask for information from the subcontractor or manufacturer involved with the reported item. These sources may have more knowledge and offer an alternative repair or acceptable explanation. Judgment calls are inevitable, and occasionally every builder gives something away.

Response

The response step consists of providing the customer with a repair or issuing a denial. If an item is to be repaired, the most efficient procedure is to issue a written *service order* (Figure 6-16). Requests for service builders telephone in to subs are too easily lost, forgotten, or misunderstood. Adequate tracking is nearly impossible and the builder has no written record for the warranty file. An employee who was not part of the original conversation but who later gets involved has no easy way of discovering what has already been done.

The written service order saves confusion and duplication of effort, provides subs with complete information, and documents work for the builder's permanent records. Most important, the customer is more likely to receive the required repair without a hassle.

Having the service order form printed on four-part NCR paper works very well. The first two copies are sent to the sub, the third is retained by the builder, and the last is sent to the homeowner. Using different colored sheets makes the destination of each copy readily identifiable.

Scheduling the work. The responsibility for contacting the homeowner for a service appointment should rest with the sub. Involving a third party in the communication only makes a difficult task more difficult and offers a myriad of opportunities for messages to be tangled up. The builder, who paid the sub to perform the original work correctly, has already inspected the item and performed the administrative chore of issuing the service order. Subs who complain that they are not near a telephone should be told diplomatically and pleasantly that this is not an acceptable excuse. This a matter of business responsibility. If the sub has made a conscientious effort and the homeowner has been unreachable, however, the sub should be able to call on the builder's staff to assist. Routine reliance on a builder's office per-

Figure 6-16: Sample Service Order
(Three-part form.)

Warranty Service Order

Date_____   Community_____

Work Order #_____   Lot #_____

Purchase Order #_____   Model_____

Contractor_____   Homeowner_____

Address_____   Address_____

_____   _____

Phone_____   (home)_____

                                (work)_____

Work Required:

                        Authorized by:_____

Comments on work performed:

        Completed by_____ Date_____

To the Contractor:
The Homeowner has received a copy of this service order and will expect to hear from you within five (5) days. Upon completion of the work, sign and return one copy for the warranty file. Your attention and cooperation are appreciated!

To the Homeowner:
To expedite setting an appointment for repair work, you may wish to contact the subcontractor listed above. If you have any questions, please call our office.

sonnel to perform this part of the sub's work is an uncalled-for expense for the builder, and the time spent doing this slows the general pace of service for all homeowners. When the repair work has been completed, the sub should sign and date the service order, then return one copy to the builder.

A homeowner might say during a Wednesday inspection, "I'm home until noon on Thursdays. Can you just tell everyone to come in the morning?" The answer, again given diplomatically and in a friendly tone, is no. The builder can offer to put a note on the service order that the customer is available for service appointments on Thursday mornings. This statement should be followed by a brief (and patient) description of the service order process and the reasons for putting everything in writing. This also is an excellent time to mention that the customer is welcome to expedite the process by initiating the call to the sub once the service order has been received. Contact between the homeowner and sub at that point is quite acceptable. If customers respond that they do not see this as their job, the builder can agree, indicating that it was only a suggestion to make scheduling more convenient for the homeowner. A thorough description of warranty procedures in the homeowner manual often can prevent this problem.

A good case can be made by customers that they bought the home from the builder, the defects should not be there, and they should not be bothered talking to service people. In principle, this is a valid point. In practical reality, it does not eliminate the communication problem. At the same time, hiring someone to sit by the telephone all day and make all the necessary calls would force the builder to charge more for each home. Even that would not eliminate the possibility of mixing up appointments or last minute changes. Having the customer and the sub speak directly to each other is the safest scheduling method for all concerned.

If the builder feels an obligation to provide this extra service, the staffing needs to meet the commitment must be considered. Even making one call to each party would be a time-consuming activity. Unfortunately, the builder's employee will seldom connect with both parties on the first try. Messages must be recorded accurately, and often half a dozen calls will occur before the appointment is set. And often that appointment will be changed, sometimes at the last minute. It is admirable for builders to want to manage this process, but if it is to be done successfully, the builder must accept the cost right along with the responsibility. Otherwise, the builder risks creating a customer expectation that won't be fulfilled.

Multiple-trade Repairs. The classic example of a multiple-trade repair is a plumbing leak that has damaged dry wall and will therefore require subs from at least three different trades to correct. If the normal time frame for service order completion is fourteen days, the homeowner needing a multiple-trade repair could wait six to eight weeks for all the paperwork and service to be completed. How can the builder coordinate all the parts of this service to accomplish the job within the normal time frame?

All the service orders for the repair should be issued at one time, with only the first one dated. Each service order should list the specific repair at the top and include instructions to notify the builder or the next subcontractor *immediately* upon completion of the work. Subcontractors down the line should be notified to expect a call when the job is ready for them. For this example, the plumber's service order could read, "(1) repair leak in wall behind master shower, and (2) notify 'Straight Walls' drywall immediately at (telephone number) when work is finished." Similarly, the drywall company's service order would list the specific follow-up work, note to expect a call from the plumber, and instruct that the *next* sub (if any) be notified upon completion of the drywall work. The date the plumbing is repaired thus becomes the date the drywall company's service order is activated, and so forth.

If subs' reliability in carrying this step through is questionable, builders can instruct that they be notified at each step—or they can tentatively schedule each trade when issuing the service orders, follow up to track completion of each step, and make a confirming call to the next service technician in line.

Depending on the personality of the customer and on the customer's relationship with the builder, some homeowners may be willing to assume responsibility for notifying subs. Such customers appreciate it if the builder will outline at the beginning what the repair steps will be, mentioning in particular any procedures that require more than one visit. Customers who know what to expect are less likely to lose patience while waiting for yet another sub to arrive. Steady progress combined with the assurance that someone is monitoring the work will usually keep customers satisfied.

Special situations occur relatively infrequently, so they should not create serious problems for anyone involved. Common sense dictates that the goal is to get the defect corrected and related repairs done as quickly as possible for the customer, preferably within the normal time frame. By alerting the subcontractors to any special circumstances, the builder helps ensure their cooperation. Situations such as this offer the subs a chance to demonstrate their appreciation of the builder by absorbing minor back charges.

Working in Occupied Homes. Whenever a builder or builder's representatives are in a home, even if the homeowner is present, the builder has a responsibility and a liability. Damage to counter tops, floor coverings, or other items caused by tool boxes, dirty shoes, mistakes, or accidents should be corrected. The builder is responsible for intervening on behalf of the customer. Any discussion with the service person involved is a private matter between the builder and that individual. The homeowner should not be bothered with it but should only see quick and effective correction of the damage.

This responsibility increases if children and pets live in the home. A child who gets hurt playing with a tool or a pet that escapes while service people are entering or leaving the home quickly becomes the builder's problem. If a stereo disappears on the day that three subs use the homeowner's key, it becomes the builder's problem. Regardless of what the homeowner may have signed in the way of a release or authorization to enter the home, the builder is ethically (and in most states, legally) liable for such occurrences. This responsibility should never be taken lightly. Only individuals who are completely trustworthy should be sent into homes, whether or not the homeowner is present.

Tracking Completions. While the work proceeds, the builder's copy of the service order is filed in a special notebook, or sometimes on computer. A very workable manual system can be set up as follows: a three-ring binder, indexed by trade, is kept on or near the desk of the individual responsible for tracking service orders. Tabs labeled for each trade or subcontractor are included; a "miscellaneous" section accommodates service orders to subs who rarely receive warranty assignments.

Each tabbed category contains a service order log (Figure 6-17). New service orders are noted on the log, which is kept in the front of the appropriate section for tracking. Daily, any completed orders received by the builder are matched to the builder's file copy and the completion date is noted on the log. The builder copy then can be removed and thrown away; the signed and dated subcontractor copy is filed in the appropriate warranty file.

After recording and removing completed orders, the person who tracks the service order checks those remaining in the notebook to determine if any have expired or are about to. A

Figure 6-17: Sample Work Order Log

Work Order Log

Contractor_____   Phone_____

Date		Work Order #	Name of Homeowner	Comment/Completion Date
Issued	Expires			

telephone call to the sub and possibly to the affected homeowner usually provides information as to the reason for the delay. This alerts everyone that the builder is aware of the outstanding work. Homeowners often are relieved to hear from the builder. Subs become more responsive when they realize someone is tracking these items.

Notes can be made directly on the builder's copy. If the comments are significant, the builder may want to staple this copy to the sub's completed copy and keep both in the warranty file when the work is finished.

Once subs become accustomed to this level of involvement from the builder, they will begin to call with an update if a service order is slow in being completed. This eliminates the need for the builder's call, and noting the update on the builder copy allows anyone to check the status of the service request. It never hurts for the builder to contact the homeowner affected to confirm that the customer knows the latest status. This reassures the homeowner that the builder is monitoring the work.

Another tracking system that works well if the volume is small is placing incomplete orders on a bulletin board and reviewing them daily. If the number is small, a quick glance will identify any that require builder intervention. As service orders are completed, they are removed and filed. Anyone who comes into the office can readily see the amount of warranty work waiting to be performed. This visibility can be an advantage or a disadvantage, depending on who's doing the looking and why. The plumber with two outstanding service orders may point to an expired order for the cabinet company and use their slow performance to defend his own, claiming "everybody's doing it." Every warranty processing choice carries implications for other activities; builders should carefully consider what will work best in *their* situation.

Warranty Denial. Four recognized categories of repair items are usually denied warranty service. Generally builders will not provide repair for an item that

- resulted from homeowner damage (Figure 6-18),
- is out of warranty through passage of time (Figure 6-19),
- is outside the scope of the warranty (it was never covered by the warranty—see Figure 6-20), or
- falls within acceptable standards as specified in the warranty by the builder or by industry standards (Figure 6-21).

Saying no to a customer usually is as uncomfortable for the builder as it is for the customer. The builder does not want to alienate the customer or end up with a conflict. The homeowner requested, and therefore obviously wants, the repair.

Setting limits on acceptable work is inevitable. When the customer requests repairs on items that are not the builder's responsibility to correct, the customer is testing those limits. This is a natural enough process and can range from friendly to hostile in tone.

If the builder changes the limits to suit the customer, that customer will thereafter believe that exceptions to the standards are possible. So will that customer's neighbors and friends. At times, the builder will have good reason to "bend the rules." It is sometimes very difficult to know what the right choice is. This is a judgment call and should be made with complete recognition of the precedent it sets.

Sometimes "no" turns out *not* to be the correct answer. The customer's description of a problem may be inaccurate and mislead someone who reads the service request. Making a decision

Figure 6-18: Sample Letter of Denial, Homeowner Damage

Background: The name of the landscape firm used by the builder was given to two elderly sisters (note the form of address used in the inside address). The landscape company was slow in responding to such a "small" assignment. After four weeks, hearing nothing, the homeowners called to ask when the work would be done. The landscape company's office manager became defensive and rude, making several comments about them expecting too much and being out of touch with reality. The builder provided a bit of extra service to regain some good will, but still wanted to make it clear that maintaining good drainage is the homeowner's responsibility. A copy of this letter was sent to the landscaping sub to reinforce the message the builder already had expressed by phone to the owner of the landscape firm. The builder shortly thereafter replaced the landscaping sub; the sub's owner had seemed to understand customer service, but the employees were somehow not getting the message.

(Builder Logo)

August 17, 199X

Mmes. Mary & Virginia Samson
(Address)

Dear Mmes. Samson:

This is to confirm our recent conversations regarding the erosion in your backyard.

The (Builder's Company Name) has issued a service order to (Builder's Service Technician) to fill the area where soil has washed away, especially at the edge of the patio slab.

As we discussed, this erosion is unavoidable while the area remains unlandscaped. By installing your landscaping you will protect the concrete patio and prevent other damage to the finish grade. Water is expected to drain through this area from the neighboring lot but should be able to do so without causing damage once the surface is covered with sod or rock.

Our service order to refill this area is provided as a courtesy to you and will be our last attention to this item. We understand your frustration with the slow response of the landscape company and therefore have made this contribution to assist you in getting the matter resolved.

On behalf of (Builder's Company Name) and (Landscaping Subcontractor) I want to apologize for the treatment you received from a contractor that we introduced to you. Discourtesy to a customer is not acceptable under any circumstances and even less so when the customer has been so patient. I regret that you were upset by very unprofessional and completely inexcusable remarks. (Landscape Subcontractor) has assured me your work will be completed this week.

Please call me if I can be of any further assistance.

Sincerely,

(Signature)
Warranty Manager

cc: (Landscaping Subcontractor)

Figure 6-19: Sample Letter of Denial, Out of Warranty

Whether to address a homeowner as "Mr.", "Ms.," or "Mrs." is a question best decided on a case-by-case basis. If conversations include first names, it is usually acceptable to use the first name(s) in letters. When in doubt, use the more formal form of address. It is better to be more formal than necessary than risk offending a customer with familiarity.

(Builder Logo)

March 18, 199X

Mr. Arnold Smythe
(Address)

Dear Mr. Smythe:

This is to confirm our conversation of March 16, 199X, regarding the status of your limited warranty.

As I explained, the materials and workmanship warranty on your new home was for one year, beginning the day of closing, January 17, 199X (previous year). Accordingly, the warranty for your home expired as of January 17 of this year.

We will complete the service orders that have been issued in response to items you reported in writing during the warranty and which we agreed were covered by the warranty. Since these address exterior items they will not be completed until weather conditions improve. As we discussed in our meeting, the fact that work on these items is still pending does not affect the status of the limited warranty with regard to other items.

Any additional work that is required to maintain your home is now your responsibility. We will be happy to provide you with information you might need to accomplish repairs. However, it is now up to you to arrange, schedule, and pay for such work.

I hope this clears up any misunderstanding or confusion that might have existed.

Sincerely,

(Signature)
Warranty Manager

---

without being certain of all the facts can be embarrassing for the builder. Such embarrassment can be avoided by making it a practice to understand exactly what is requested and why the customer feels justified in expecting the repair.

This kind of customer service decision can not be made sitting behind a desk: inspecting the item and investigating other sources of information are critical steps in the process.

If the builder's final response *is* no, this information is best delivered in person. The next best way is by telephone. Hearing

Figure 6-20: Sample Letter of Denial, Outside the Scope of Warranty

Copying this letter to the landscape sub and the management company provides a professional touch by answering the question, "Who else needs to know?" The effort may also forestall the need for either of those companies to call and ask the status of the work if they hear from Mr. K.

(Builder logo)

July 31, 199X

Mr. Isaac Katzbetson
(Address)

Dear Mr. Katzbetson:

In response to your phone call of July 30, I have reviewed all information related to the tree in your front yard and inspected the tree myself this morning.

We sincerely regret that you are experiencing a problem with the tree. However, as stated in the landscaping information which you received when you purchased your home, the (Builder Company) warranty does not include plant material.

Many factors such as disease, insects, weather, and soil conditions over which no one has control can impact the success of newly established landscaping. Past experience has shown that a common problem with trees is the "weedeater" type of trimmer, which can destroy the bark and consequently kill the tree. This appears to be the problem with your tree.

The warranty on plant materials is direct to you from the original landscaper, (Name of Subcontractor). That warranty in turn provides that replacement will be made one time.

Since this tree was replaced in response to a walk through in August, 19XX, (Landscape Subcontractor) has no further obligation. At this point in time, replacing the tree is a homeowner maintenance responsibility.

If you wish to enlist the help of (Landscape Subcontractor) in replacing the tree, you can contact them directly at _____-_____. The service manager is (Name); they are open Monday through Friday from 7:00 a.m. until 5:00 p.m. and Saturdays from 8:00 a.m. until 1:00 p.m.

Although the (Builder's Company Name) is not responsible for replacing the tree, if we can assist you by providing any additional information, we will be happy to do so.

Sincerely,

(Signature)
Warranty Manager

cc: (Management Company for townhome community)
(Landscape Subcontractor)

Figure 6-21: Sample Letter of Denial, Difference in Standards

This letter promptly documents the understanding arrived at during a meeting, before memory is distorted by interpretation. If any of the subjects come up again, a record exists from which to renew discussion.

(Builder Logo)

August 16, 199X

Mr. & Ms. Robert McRey
(Address)

Dear Bob and Mary:

This is to confirm our conversation of August 15, 1990, regarding warranty services pending on your home. Copies of service orders for work which we have agreed should be performed in your home are enclosed.

One of the items addressed is sealing around the air conditioning line at the point where it enters your home. We believe this will resolve the complaint of the bath being cold, but recognize that until cold weather occurs you cannot confirm this.

The repair to the master tub is currently being scheduled with Ace Porcelain Repair for August 20. The repair will take most of one day to complete; the tub will be usable beginning the following morning, and the work will carry a one-year warranty.

Another item discussed in our meeting was the cracking/settling of your driveway. Two cracks, one ⅛″ in width (no displacement) and a second that is hairline to 1/16″ (no displacement) have developed in the lower half of the drive.

As described in the warranty documents, concrete cracking of this type is often caused by shrinkage and minor soil movement. The damage to your drive is typical and within our written warranty standards.

We have agreed to caulking these cracks in the driveway. Under the terms of the warranty, this service is provided one time and thereafter maintenance of the concrete slabs is a homeowner responsibility.

I regret the misunderstanding we have experienced over these matters. We believe that our warranty literature is clear and forthright.

While I recognize that some of the normal industry standards included in it do not meet your personal standards, these were the terms of our agreement with you at the time our contract was signed. It is our sincere intention to fulfill our warranty obligations as defined by these documents.

Sincerely,

(Signature)
Warranty Manager

Enclosures

nothing for three weeks and then receiving an impersonal letter denying service would upset any homeowner. At any rate, the customer must be told of the decision: hearing, "I'll check on this and get back to you . . ." and then never hearing another word on the subject can lead to disaster.

Customers hear a loud "maybe" when such comments are made and they will not forget the comment or the item. While in some cases a bit of extra investigation may be required for the decision, using this comment *as an exit line* always backfires. When such a comment is necessary, make the follow-through specific: "I'll get back to you Friday afternoon." The builder can further suggest, "if you haven't heard from me by 4:00 p.m. Friday, please call me." Even if no definite answer has been determined, the promised call must be made. It is always better for the builder to initiate contact than to wait for a frustrated homeowner to call back. The homeowner who must place the call, feeling ignored or forgotten, will be angry even before hearing the builder's answer. Builders can spare themselves and their customers this extra aggravation by responding promptly to requests.

When saying no to a customer, one of the builder's goals will be to ensure that the customer feels appreciated, respected, and fairly treated. Offering an explanation and help in finding more information can soften the customer's sense of rejection or helplessness (see Figures 6-19 and 6-20). If extra service has been provided, the warranty service representative should call attention to that fact in a matter of fact way, so that the builder receives the deserved credit. Gently emphasizing that this is above and beyond what's required can also mitigate the potential damage from setting a precedent of changing the rules.

Patience, calm reason, and the understanding that the homeowner need not like the builder's answer are all helpful attitudes when rejecting a service request. Courtesy is always in order, even if the repair requested is not. Chapter 8 includes specific tips for handling situations that may involve conflict.

Some customers seem to make excessive demands for no more substantial reason than believing that the world owes them whatever they want. It is the builder's job to make decisions based on objective facts and physical conditions. The builder need not guess about the customer's motivation or try to improve the customer's personality (however tempting that might be). It is okay to say no to a customer. It is never okay to be rude about it.

The final step in responding to a homeowner request with a denial is to put the information in writing, preferably in a letter to the homeowner. "This is to confirm our conversation regarding . . ." is a very useful phrase when writing such letters. This last step can prevent the homeowner from submitting the item again three months later (or if the customer hears that someone new has taken over warranty service). A copy should go to the warranty file and to any sub related to the item. A builder will handle hundreds of such documents and may only need one of them in a legal situation. Should a serious conflict arise, however, having that one will make handling all the others suddenly worthwhile.

Follow-up

Monitoring completion of service orders through a regular reporting system is fine. The resulting information is instrumental in deciding whom to hire for future work. But it does not substitute for daily or at least weekly checking of outstanding service orders. Sending an unpleasant note to a sub who has fourteen 65-day-old service orders is taking too little action too late in the game. Even a good reporting system is no substitute for quick service intervention.

Builders and remodelers should beware of computer reports that conveniently "age" service orders. It does no one any good for the builder to know that some of the service orders are over 90 days old. Having such a category in a computer report implies that this condition is normal and to be expected. It should be neither.

This does not, however, invalidate the use of computer automation in warranty. Databases and word processing systems on computers are excellent tools to support warranty work and can considerably speed the processing of routine paperwork. The important thing is to remember that the computer is only a tool; while it can generate useful data, it cannot make decisions, establish policy, or "solve" procedural problems. If a builder has established a sensible warranty process, computers can be an excellent way to make that system work more efficiently.

When a service order exceeds its time limit the builder should immediately take steps to correct the situation. Any service work that is excessively or consistently behind warrants serious scrutiny from the builder: perhaps the builder needs to replace certain subcontractors. If a valid reason exists for uncompleted work, the service order should be placed on hold until it is appropriate to reactivate it or it should be canceled and reissued at a later date.

Calls to Confirm Satisfaction. "While I've got you on the phone . . ." is probably the most often cited reason builders hate to call homeowners to check on their satisfaction with work that has been done. Those calls, however, can make all the difference and put the builder's reputation in a class by itself.

A simple and effective response to this constantly repeated remark is needed. With some practice, the warranty rep can gracefully interrupt the customer and ask if any of the new items are emergencies. If the customer says they are not, the warranty rep then can respond, "I'll be happy to go through them with you if you have some questions, but I will be able to set an inspection and get these items processed for you as soon as we receive your written report of them. Do you have a service request form or would you like me to mail one to you?" Again, the best solution is to ensure that the request goes through the builder's established warranty system.

Especially for significant repairs such as plumbing, electrical, and heating, or replacement of a major item, a call to confirm that the job was done completely and correctly provides a professional level of service. If the customer is dissatisfied, it is far better that the builder hear it than neighbors or friends. As with rejections of service requests, complaints about the quality of repair work can not be resolved from behind a desk. An inspection appointment should be set involving the customer, the builder, and the service person, sub/owner, or manufacturer. Even if it turns out that nothing more can (or should) be done, the customer will appreciate the builder's effort to resolve the situation.

Permanent Records. Homeowner warranty files should contain a copy of the walk-through, color selection sheet, homeowner requests for service, inspection reports, signed work orders, letters denying service, and any other correspondence or records of phone calls. Photographs, diagrams, and other material related to warranty work should be carefully maintained in chronological order. If each new item is dated and placed in the front of the file, any subsequent reader can easily review the history of service on the home.

Once the home is out of warranty, the file can be removed and stored separately. Expired warranties should, however, be stored within easy reach. A colored highlighter can be used to mark the file label for homes with expired warranties. In this way, a file that is removed for some other reason can quickly be returned to the correct place. Searching through three file cabinets only to find an "out of warranty" file mixed in with the current files is unnecessary work.

If available storage space allows, it is helpful to keep "expired" files accessible for at least a year after the warranty period is over. Ultimately, the warranty file can be stored with the contract/closing file. Because warranties are legal documents, they should be subject to a planned retention policy the builder develops in consultation with a qualified attorney. In developing such a retention policy, it is helpful to know how long implied warranties are considered to be in effect in all states where the builder is active.

Should a real estate agent or potential second buyer contact a builder for the warranty history of a particular home, a cautious response is appropriate. If the builder generously forwards copies of all such records and the sale falls through because of something thus revealed, the original owner might be upset. On the other hand, real estate law requires disclosure. Still, the builder does not own the home. The safest response is to state that the builder "will be happy to comply with the request as soon as written authorization from the owner of record is received."

Monitoring Feedback

Service performance should be checked regularly against the builder's goals. This must include obtaining comments from customers. Although the numbers may look good on the monthly reports, if the customers perceive that service is slow, unfriendly, or of poor quality, the builder will have a poor image. Additionally, changing markets may change the priorities for service. Being sensitive to subtle shifts in the market allows the builder to respond quickly with program adjustments. The only effective way to accomplish this is by hearing the opinions and impressions of real live customers.

A written survey (Figure 6-22) is a good starting point. Mailing a survey between the third and sixth month of ownership allows the customer time to have become settled and probably to have experienced some warranty service. The survey should be followed by telephone calls to homeowners who did not respond; no one should be left out of this process.

Interviewing homeowners in their home can be time consuming, but this is a great way to get feedback. If such interviews become routine, they need not be a burden; for example, the builder might select two customer files at random once a month.

Figure 6-22: Sample Homeowner Survey

Homeowner Survey

We'd like to ask your opinion . . .

We are sincerely interested in your comments regarding both our product and service. Please take a few minutes to complete the questions below and return this sheet in the enclosed stamped/addressed envelope.

1. Why did you select one of our homes?

   ☐ Reputation   ☐ Referral   ☐ Construction quality

   ☐ Location   ☐ Financing   ☐ Neighborhood

   ☐ Features/appliances ☐ Price   ☐ Options/upgrades

   ☐ Size   ☐ Realtor

   ☐ Floor plan   ☐ Other_____

2. Based on the quality of the home and service we've provided would you buy another home from us?

   ☐ yes   ☐ no   ☐ undecided

3. Would you recommend our homes to others?

   ☐ yes   ☐ no   ☐ undecided

4. Please RATE our	Excellent	Good	Fair	Poor	Comment
Sales personnel					
Design/floor plan					
Constr. quality					
Walk-through					
Warranty service					
Total performance					

5. Have our personnel treated you in a courteous and professional manner?

   _____

   _____

6. Please add any other comments about your home, our company, product, personnel, or service.

   _____

   _____

   _____

Thank You! Your feedback is most valuable to us in improving our product and service. Your signature is requested but not required—

   _____

Once a year, a focus group involving three to six customers will generate much interest and excitement. The ideas generated will range from insightful and practical to hilarious and absurd. Still, no one is in a better position to tell the builder what it is like doing business with the company than the people who have done business with the company. The builder who is not listening has no chance to hear this rich and valuable input.

SUCCESSFUL SUBCONTRACTOR RELATIONSHIPS

Subcontractors provide a significant portion of new home warranty service. Even if a builder's employees are very service conscious, if one or more subs are not, the builder's reputation will suffer.

The Subcontractor as the Builder

Many customers misunderstand the relationship between the builder and the subs. Even those who do understand often conclude that because the builder hired the sub, he or she endorses the sub's behavior and work performance. For most customers, the subs *are* the builder. Their performance is a direct reflection on the builder's reputation. Customers apply the same criteria to a sub's performance as they apply to the builder's staff: response time, attitude, and ability. The potential impact of this on future business is too important to leave to chance.

As an independent businessperson, each subcontractor will have a distinct customer service attitude. These attitudes vary from outstanding to terrible. While technical skill and pricing may be excellent, if a sub's service is poor the home buyer and consequently the builder will suffer in the end.

A builder should consider service along with ability and price when selecting subs. When feasible, it is a good idea to begin by checking on service performance with other builders for whom the sub has worked. If some negatives are reported, the builder has the option of hiring the sub knowing what pitfalls to guard against. Even when reports are excellent, the builder's job is not yet complete.

The Builder as Customer

The builder is the customer of the subcontractor at this point. As such, the builder has a right to some expectations. These expectations need to be communicated to the subcontractor and adjusted if necessary. All points should be agreed upon by both the builder and sub in the initial stages of this relationship.

Few builders forget to discuss specifications, scheduling, and price for the work required. Payment terms are seldom overlooked; on-site supervision and the location of the job usually are thoroughly covered. These points are discussed routinely because they are important to both the builder and the sub. Adding warranty service to this list raises the topic to the same level of importance.

Too often, warranty is omitted from initial conversations when new subs are considered or hired. Terms of the warranty and specific procedures become apparent only as they are applied, usually in full view of the homeowner. Misunderstandings and disagreements occur between the builder and the subcontractor. Poor service results, and in the end no one is happy.

Preparing an agenda of warranty and service points to discuss with new subcontractors offers excellent insurance against this (see Figure 7-1). For some subs, one or more topics on the agenda may not apply and can be deleted. For example, an after-hours emergency number probably is not needed from the cabinet supplier.

Using a standardized, written agenda not only ensures that nothing is overlooked, it serves another important purpose as well. The sub who receives written guidelines about service issues immediately sees that the builder considers this a priority. When warranty and customer care are discussed on an equal basis with specs, schedules, and pricing, the significance is hard to miss. The discussion can take as little as twenty minutes or as long as two hours, but the time spent may be one of the best investments the builder makes on behalf of the company's service reputation.

To further emphasize this priority, a builder can ask that the individuals directly responsible for service attend the meeting. If the sub's owners are not involved in daily service work, this is an excellent way to be certain that those who are have met the builder's representatives and that all parties hear the same information. Any questions that come up can be answered immediately.

Figure 7-1: Subcontractor Service Agenda

Subcontractor Service Agenda

Contractor _____   Contact _____

Address _____   Phone _____

_____   Emergency service
                                               required? _____

	Notes:
• Why care about service?	
• (Builder's) customer philosophy	
• Terms of warranty coverage 　—Period of coverage 　—Warranty standards	
• Service procedures: 　—Homeowner reports of warranty items 　　(nonemergency/emergency items) 　—Builder Inspection 　—Service order (sample copy) 　—Purchase orders for service work 　—Additional items 　—Time frame 　—Signatures 　—Return paperwork 　—Complaints about quality of repair work	
• Professionalism 　—Appointments and promptness 　—Courtesy 　—Clean up 　—Customer uncooperative/unavailable 　—Work of other trades 　—Discretion/Confidentiality	
• Back Charges	
• Late service work	
• Special procedures needed by the sub	
• Other	

The Subcontractor's Service Agenda

A wise builder will approach discussions about warranty and service form the sub's point of view. What's in it for the sub? Subcontractors are like other people; they are motivated by concern for their own well-being and goals. If subs see how providing good service to homeowners will benefit their business, the subs are more likely to be enthusiastic. Several points can be brought out in discussions to promote this perspective. Most obvious, perhaps, is the fact that if a sub's performance is successful, the builder is more likely to hire them again.

Just as important, the better the builder's reputation, the more sales the builder will make. This means more potential work for the sub, perhaps even providing much-needed security in slower times. Being associated with a builder who has a fine reputation benefits the sub when bidding other jobs or attracting new employees. And day-to-day work is more enjoyable when customers are satisfied. No one wants to go to work to hear continual complaints and threats.

Real, long-term benefits accrue to the sub in return for making a positive contribution to the builder's service reputation. Too often, builders and subs alike lose sight of this "big picture." A moment spent refocusing on this larger perspective can result in a fresh service commitment from the sub.

Sharing Customer Philosophy

The builder should share the company's customer service philosophy with each sub hired. Although the builder's philosophy may vary somewhat from the subcontractor's personal view, the sub's obligation when working for a builder is to represent the builder's philosophy. If the sub's and the builder's perspective are so different that working together will be uncomfortable, discovering that fact early can prevent problems.

Terms of Warranty Coverage

In addition to carefully discussing service philosophy, the builder should provide subs an opportunity to review a copy of the builder warranty. By doing so, subcontractors can plan their own work in response to service requests. The review should cover basic conditions and procedures.

Length of Coverage. A year is a year is a year . . . . But what if the subcontractor starts the warranty year the day he installs equipment and the builder starts it the day of closing? Then "a year" can become an argument. For example, when the contractor says, "The garage door has been on that house for sixteen months" and the builder says, "Yes, but the homeowner has only been in the house for ten months and the door is messed up," an aggravating disagreement over who will pay for the adjustment can ensue. Meanwhile, the homeowner waits for service.

To keep things simple, the builder will prefer that the one-year materials and workmanship warranty begin on the day of closing for *all* subcontractors, just as it does for the builder. The warranty's starting date is important enough to be documented in the agreement between the builder and the subcontractor (Figure 7-2). If the sub is aware of this obligation when preparing a bid for work, all will be thought fair. Although some builders may argue that subs will raise bids to protect themselves from this "extra" liability, the confusion that can result from trying to track each installation merits a few extra dollars up front. This containable expense is better than risking an unmeasured liability during the last few months, when the customer has warranty coverage left but the builder does not. Besides, if all subs are bidding under this same condition, it should not matter in the end; natural competition will keep bid increases to a minimum.

Warranty Standards

Each subcontractor should have an opportunity to review the commitment being made to the customer in terms of any extras that will be provided. Written standards that form the basis of insured warranties offer an excellent way to cover this. Many builders who do not use insured warranty coverage have developed their own written standards for their work. These are based on industry standards and vary only slightly from builder to builder. Also, even with written standards, there are judgment calls. It is impossible to anticipate every potential defect that might show up. But well-written standards covering typical situations will provide a good framework for making decisions in exceptional cases.

Most builders go a bit beyond what is legally required of them in caring for homes during the first year. Depending on the subcontractor and the particular service under discussion, it may be simpler to include such extras as part of the work described in the subcontractor agreement. If the sub and the builder have cultivated a strong mutual understanding of warranty standards, the sub will be more likely to cooperate with the builder on the occasional judgment calls. The paint contractor may automatically assign a specified number of hours of touch-up for each floor plan and incorporate that into the pricing. This eliminates

---

Figure 7-2: Sample Agreement, Warranty Clause

WARRANTY. Contractor agrees to perform all Work in a first-class, workmanlike manner. Work shall at least be equal to the HUD/FHA Minimum Property Standards, in accordance with all Municipal, County, and State building codes, and in accordance with the terms and dates as outlined in the Company limited warranty, a copy of which is attached and by reference made part of this agreement.

Unless otherwise specified herein, Contractor guarantees the work against all defects of materials and workmanship for a period of one year from the date of the certificate of occupancy as issued by the governmental agency having jurisdiction over the construction. This warranty shall be in addition to all other rights and privileges which the Company may have under any other law. Neither the final payment nor any provision in the contract documents shall relieve the Contractor of responsibility for faulty materials or workmanship.

Contractor shall remedy, at its sole cost and expense, any defects due to its faulty materials or workmanship and pay for any damage to other work or materials resulting therefrom, within fifteen (15) working days after being notified by the Company.

In an emergency, as defined in the Company limited warranty documents, notification of the Contractor will be by telephone with a written service order to follow.

_____ Contractor shall provide a 24-hour emergency telephone number and service
_____ 24-hour emergency telephone number and service not required

Contractor will be notified of nonemergency items by written service order. Service order forms indicating the completion of remedial work must be signed and dated by the Contractor or the Contractor's representative who performs the work, and returned to the Company. Until the signed service order is received in the Company office, the work will be considered to be incomplete.

The Company retains the right to assign remedial work that is not completed within the established time frame to another contractor and charge the cost of such work to Contractor. Adequate funds may be retained at the Company's option, from any payments then due to Contractor until all remedial work over fifteen (15) days old is completed.

This sample is provided for purposes of illustration only. When developing or revising warranty documents or other legal documents, always have them reviewed by an attorney qualified for the state(s) in which they will be used.

the need for tracking minute amounts of time here and there and assumes that, overall, everyone comes out even. An unusual circumstance could easily be handled separately with a purchase order. The drywall contractor should be aware of what the builder expects in relation to repairing normal shrinkage cracks that occur in most new homes. Tile installers will want to understand their obligation to repair grout cracks, and so on. Many workable builder-subcontractor arrangements are possible. Good information about how often such work should be expected is essential for fair calculation and pricing. Mutual trust and clear communication up front are key to this kind of working relationship. It may take several years to reach this point with some subcontractors.

Service Procedures

The builder's service procedures translate service philosophy into practical activities. Though the sub may not be directly involved in some of the steps, the sub should be aware of how the builder handles service requests from start to finish. Knowing that the builder has organized an entire program to handle warranty and service items reinforces the importance of service work in the mind of the subcontractor.

The sub who feels he or she is being sent to homes haphazardly or frivolously may find it difficult to take service orders seriously. However, if the sub knows that the customer reports nonemergency items in writing and that the builder's representative inspects the items to confirm the legitimacy of the claim, prompt attention is more likely.

The subcontractor and the builder should have the same understanding of what constitutes an emergency (see chapter 6) and whether 24-hour, seven day service is required. This detail also is important enough to be documented in the subcontractor agreement (Figure 7-2).

The question of whether to permit or encourage homeowners to contact subs directly must be decided by each builder. The success of such a system requires that the subs be adept at handling service items and that builder and subs share a high degree of trust. Turnover among subcontractors, excessive numbers of problems, or a product line that appeals to buyers unwilling to administer their own warranty work can turn such a program into a disaster for homeowners and builders. Subs lose the advantage of having the builder screen claims. A more common practice is to supply homeowners with off-hour emergency numbers for critical subs (heat, electric, plumbing) and maintain direct involvement in all other warranty claims.

Builder Inspection. Screening warranty items by inspecting them prior to issuing service orders saves subs time and provides more accurate and complete information. The builder also benefits from seeing problems firsthand. Recurring problems are more readily identified and all involved can feel more confident that the appropriate sub is being sent to the home. The homeowner who reports cracked tile may have cracked tile, but often it is the grout rather than the tile that is cracked. This kind of information can determine whom the sub sends to perform the repair.

Furthermore, cracked tiles that resulted from a crowned joist could be repaired only after the joist was repaired. Wasting subcontractors' time by issuing inappropriate or unnecessary service orders breeds disrespect, erodes service, and tarnishes the long-term business relationship between builder and subs.

Service Orders and Purchase Orders. Providing the sub with a sample copy of a service order can prevent confusion and delays later. The sub seeing a service order for the first time may have no idea what procedure the builder expects in response. A minute or two spent reviewing a sample can speed the response process later, when a real service order is sent. A clause in the subcontractor agreement can explain how the builder will provide notice to the sub regarding warranty items (see Figure 7-2).

Subcontractors are familiar with standard purchase order forms authorizing initial installations. On occasion, the builder may need to issue a purchase order for warranty service work. A sub's special skills are sometimes needed to repair damage unrelated to the sub's original workmanship or materials. Understanding that he or she is not expected to stand the cost of repairing the drywall that was damaged by a plumbing leak will keep the drywall contractor happy and produce quicker service for the homeowner. In emergency situations, a purchase order number given over the phone can instigate repair activity while the paperwork catches up. The subcontractor should be made aware who in the builder's organization has the authority to issue purchase orders for service work.

Additional Items. Homeowners often report new warranty items to the service person who arrives to work in the home. Builders usually have a policy that states that subs will not be paid for work they perform unless it has been authorized by the builder. Yet the additional item the homeowner reports may be a legitimate warranty matter for which the sub is responsible. It makes little sense to the sub to refer the homeowner to the builder only to be sent back out to the same home to repair the item a week later. The added inconvenience to the homeowner also can make the builder's system look foolish or inconsiderate.

In some cases, it is just common sense to have the sub repair the item in the same visit. Using a "ten-minute" rule can help: If the additional item can be repaired in ten minutes, the sub should do the work, noting it on the original service order so that it is documented for the warranty file. If the work is extensive, would make the sub late for the next appointment, involves other subcontractors, or if there is any question whether it is a legitimate warranty item, the homeowner should go through normal channels to obtain another service order.

Normal Time Frame. One of the major points builders should stress in their early conversations with subcontractors is the time frame to be observed. Again, this is important enough to be documented in the contract. By specifying an actual number of business or calendar days, little is left to interpretation (see Figure 7-2).

Many builders rely on a thirty-day time frame. This response time is inadequate for the builder seeking a reputation for superior service. In most cases, an entire home can be built in about ninety days. The homeowner will rightfully wonder why it takes a third of that time (or more) to fix a leaky faucet, adjust a door, or replace a defective light.

From the customer's point of view, service in under thirty days definitely counts in the builder's favor. Making no other changes in service, a builder can improve the company's reputation significantly simply by reducing warranty response time by a week or ten days. As discussed in chapter 6, builders should *never* promise more than they can deliver, however. Subcontractors should be required to stay within the same time limits that the builder's service personnel meet—and vice versa.

Signatures. Some service order forms include a line for the customer's signature indicating satisfaction with the work. Whether or not this requirement accomplishes anything positive in a service program is open to discussion. A customer's signature on a service order does not guarantee a satisfied customer. If a husband signs a work order but his wife is displeased, the builder (and sub) still have a problem. If both homeowners work, the practical obstacles to obtaining a signature can cause a genuine inconvenience to both the homeowner and the sub.

By requesting a signature the builder gives the customer the authority to set standards, at least temporarily. Customers who willingly sign are usually content and likely to stay that way; those who refuse often are the same customers who are difficult in other ways. Requesting signatures on completed work gives difficult customers even more leverage. Some builders report good results when they obtain homeowner signatures; others have eliminated the requirement with no ill effects.

Builders who do not require the homeowner's signature do expect the signature of the service technician who performed the work and the date it was completed. Knowing that the builder has this information on file often encourages service personnel to take special care in all aspects of their work, including cleanup and courtesy. If a homeowner complains, an adequate response is easier if the builder knows who performed the service. Whatever policy the builder follows for signatures, the policy needs to be made clear to all subs and consistently enforced.

Returning Paperwork. Whether computerized or manual, a well-planned service system will require that completed service orders be returned for the builder's permanent records on the home. Unless all subcontractors understand the importance of this detail, an otherwise effective system will deteriorate into chaos.

Most subcontractors readily cooperate with this requirement. However, occasionally a sub will be less rigorous about completing outstanding paperwork than the builder's employee who is charged with tracking the service orders. A simple policy that credit is not given for finished work until the completed paperwork is returned to the builder usually will produce the desired result. Like all the other builder policies, this must be discussed up front to avoid confusion and conflict when it is enforced.

Complaints. If a builder hears from a customer that repair work is unacceptable, a good response is to say, "I regret hearing that. What is a convenient time for me to look at this with you?" Trying to resolve such issues over the phone is a waste of time. Homeowners interpret long-winded discussions as defensive and may become more upset. Volunteering to reexamine an item shows interest without relinquishing the authority to set standards. (Hint: saying, "Well, you signed the service order . . ." will not resolve the complaint. It will, however, teach the homeowner never to sign anything again, while contributing nothing positive to the builder's relationship with the customer.)

If the subcontractor knows that a complaint from a customer will produce a visit by the builder, the sub will be more likely to pay strict attention to details and perform a sound repair. Furthermore, subs who are aware that this is the procedure for responding to complaints will not be surprised to be invited to attend such meetings from time to time. Some would even insist on it. If the complaint involves a defective product, calling in a manufacturer's representative may be helpful. Manufacturers' reps can contribute technical information and usually have the authority to replace materials at no charge if genuine problems are identified.

Professionalism

Fortunately, most subcontractors handle themselves in a very professional manner. However, it may be desirable to review the following points simply to make certain everyone is operating by the same set of rules. While some points may seem trivial or obvious, it is dangerous to assume that all the subs will practice these service basics.

Appointments and Promptness. Depending on the trade, some subs have a difficult time setting specific appointments. If the builder does not have access to the homeowner's key, or if the homeowner prefers to be present when work is done, this minor but significant detail can be an obstacle to efficient service.

Any sub should be able to make a definite appointment early in the morning. Given the often unpredictable nature of construction work, allowing the customer a range of thirty minutes such as 2:00-2:30 instead of stating a precise arrival time can forestall disappointment. Sometimes, a customer is satisfied with an "a.m." or "p.m." commitment.

For the builder with limited staff, scheduling appointments for service work to be performed by subs can turn into a time-consuming nightmare. Further, the three-way communication involved in the process offers many unnecessary opportunities to confuse messages and create problems. As discussed in chapter 6, one solution to this is to provide the sub and the homeowner with each other's phone numbers. This task is easily accomplished if both receive a copy of each service order.

The burden for setting the appointment should rest with the sub, but homeowners should feel welcome to initiate contact if they are difficult to reach. This message can be conveyed to the homeowner in the literature explaining warranty procedures (see chapter 4). A reminder can be printed on the service order form as well (see chapter 6).

Some subs use paper door hangers to expedite communications with homeowners. The hangers can be supplied by the builder, customized with the builder's logo and a space for the sub's name, telephone number, and a brief note. Smaller companies can purchase blank door hangers in small quantities from an office supply store. If the sub has telephoned a customer many times with no success, a door hanger may obtain a response. On rare occasions, a sub may need to request assistance from the builder's office staff in tracking down a homeowner for an appointment. The builder's policies should make it clear that this is the exception, not the rule.

If the customer has provided the builder with a key or if the work to be performed is all exterior, service personnel still should call to alert the customer that someone will be working at the home. Again, a door hanger can serve to confirm that someone worked in the home in the customer's absence. This calls attention to the work and allows the customer to feel more secure.

Any change in the arranged time should be communicated as soon as possible and the appointment rescheduled. A homeowner who has missed three days of work waiting for the technician to show up is likely to be unhappy no matter how well the repair work is performed. The homeowner who left the key will wonder what went wrong then he or she arrives home to find the work was not completed. The courtesy of an explanation can prevent negative reactions or calls to the builder.

If the homeowner changes the appointment, a wise sub will note this on the service order and alert the builder if the deadline for completion of the work is close.

Courtesy. Requesting that service technicians introduce themselves and shake hands with the homeowner may seem elementary, but some subs will need to be reminded that this is appropriate. Offering a business card also is a good practice; most homeowners feel more comfortable about having a stranger in their home if they know a little about the person.

The attitude repair people display when working in an occupied home makes a lasting impression on homeowners. A few moments spent in ordinary pleasantries and an enthusiastic, "can-do" approach sets a positive tone that goes a long way toward a good positive service reputation. On the other hand, chatting for half an hour before or after a five-minute repair can lead to comments such as, "No wonder it takes them so long to fix anything. They spend all their time talking." A balance between chilliness and chattiness must be maintained. The goal is to be pleasant, yet businesslike and efficient.

Cleanup. As with a scheduled appointment, cleanup after completing the work becomes a problem only when it fails to happen. Even the best repair will not please a homeowner who has to clean up when the work is finished. Cleaning up is a part of every job. Many service people carry a hand-held vacuum just for this purpose.

Other points of service etiquette include removing soiled shoes prior to going into the new home, refraining from smoking in an occupied home, and placing tool boxes or other potentially damaging items safely on a clean scrap of carpet to protect floors and counters.

Subcontractors who have paid to clean a homeowner's carpet or replace a counter top never forget to follow these suggestions.

These points apply regardless of the homeowner's personal house-keeping skills—ironically, poor housekeepers usually are the first to complain if any mess is left behind. The point is that the homeowner's personal lifestyle is his or her choice; cleaning up after working in the home is a technician's service obligation.

Handling Uncooperative Customers. Most of the time, homeowners are very happy to see service personnel and will be extremely cordial to them. From time to time, however, a customer may be belligerent and hostile, refuse to set an appointment during established hours, or set an appointment and then stand up the technician. Rarely, a customer will harass the service technician who arrives to perform assigned work.

Although an organized builder will have informed homeowners about the hours service personnel are available, a difficult customer may refuse to observe that schedule or to let anyone else have a key. Service orders for customers with this attitude often return to the builder's desk incomplete. Even faced with difficult customers, builders and subs need not engage in a service tug-of-war. The builder has a warranty obligation. The builder's willingness to fulfill it is evidenced by the issuing of the service order. And a well-written warranty obligates the home-owner to provide access so that repairs can be performed when needed (See chapter 2). Thus, there are only two options: either the builder changes the scheduled service hours or the home-owner agrees to cooperate.

One workable approach for the builder is to say, "We understand it is sometimes difficult to schedule service appointments. We'll be happy to perform this work for you. Please give us 48 (or 72, or 96—whatever is appropriate) hours' notice when you can be available." It is wise to document such conversations. Usually a notation on the service order is adequate, but in severe cases, a follow-up letter to the homeowner may produce the desired result (See Figure 7-3). The work order then can be put on hold and reactivated when the customer finds a time that is convenient for the work to be performed.

If the customer allows the sub access to the home and then engages in harassment and criticism, the sub may wish simply to leave the home and report the problem to the builder rather than permit an argument to develop. When this kind of situation occurs it is commonly because the homeowner is displeased with the method of repair to be used.

Often homeowners want an item completely replaced and will not hesitate to express their disappointment with a plan to repair the item. Gluing and clamping a delaminating door or patching a

---

Figure 7-3: Sample Letter Regarding Service Hours

(Builder Logo)

(Date)

(New Homeowner)
(Address)

Dear (Homeowner's Name):

　　Routine monitoring of service orders has called our attention to warranty work that remains incomplete on your home.

　　　　Service Order #　　　　　　　　　Subcontractor

　　　　_____　　　　　　_____

　　　　_____　　　　　　_____

　　　　_____　　　　　　_____

　　We are committed to providing you with the best possible service under the terms of our warranty. Appointments for warranty work are available between the hours of 8:00 a.m. and 4:00 p.m., Monday through Friday.
　　Please call our office or the subcontractor listed to set a service appointment. If the service hours are inconvenient for you at the present time, we will be happy to place the service orders on hold until you notify us to reactivate them.

Sincerely,

(Signature)
Warranty Manager

cc: (Subcontractors listed)

---

cut in vinyl flooring are good examples. Whether to repair or replace in such cases is a matter for the builder's judgment. The subs may have had nothing to say in the builder's final decision, but the sub may bear the homeowner's direct displeasure.

　　Builders should make it clear that while they expect outstanding warranty service and consistent courtesy from the sub, this does not include tolerating abuse. The builder's warranty obligation is to repair the item; the choice of method is the builder's. Issuing the service order proves the builder's willingness to meet the obligation. The builder can be further protected by using a follow-up letter to the homeowner summarizing all of this and reiterating that the repair is available as soon as the homeowner agrees to schedule an appointment and permit the work to be performed without interference (see Figure 7-4).

A well-written warranty gives the builder yet another option: paying the homeowner the reasonable cost of repair (See chapter 2). This alternative is a last resort and should be used very infrequently, but it provides an important safety valve. One disgruntled homeowner can delay service to half a dozen other fine customers while he or she engages in power struggles with

---

Figure 7-4: Sample Letter Regarding Builder's Choice of Repair

Customers often want a problem item replaced instead of repaired. Sometimes the builder can settle the issue by providing a new item for the homeowner, repairing the broken item and using it in another home with no further problem. When that is not an option, builders can enforce the warranty clause that allows them to choose the method of repair or make the choice to replace an item.

(Builder Logo)

(Date)

(New Homeowner)
(Address)

Dear (Homeowner's Name):

In response to your request, service order #_____ was issued on _____.

The service order provides for repair of an interior door that has delaminated. This repair has been performed in the past with excellent results. We are confident that this work will meet or exceed the standards specified in the warranty documents and normal for the home building industry.

Although the choice of a method of repair is specifically reserved for the Company by the terms of the warranty, you have the option of correcting the item as part of home maintenance if you prefer.

The service technician assigned to complete this work will contact you during the next several days to arrange an appointment during normal service hours.

If you decide to proceed with another method of repair, simply inform him and we will cancel the service order and consider this matter resolved.

Please feel free to call me to discuss this if you have any concerns about the intended work or our procedures.

Sincerely,

(Signature)
Warranty Manager

cc: (Service technician or subcontractor)

builder and sub alike. A reasonable level of effort is to make three legitimate attempts to perform the repair. The builder should record and refer to the dates and actions taken in trying to provide the work in a cover letter that accompanies the check to the homeowner (see Figure 7-5).

The subcontractor should understand that the builder has the final authority regarding such options. Also genuine effort must be put forth to provide the needed repairs. Calling and getting a busy signal does not constitute a legitimate attempt. And a subcontractor should not be permitted to advise the builder to "pay

---

Figure 7-5: Sample Letter with Check in Lieu of Repair

This type of correspondence often brings a telephone call from the homeowner, who now wants to set another appointment. If the builder arranges an appointment and the homeowner fails to keep it, the letter should then be firmly enforced. (Builders should be certain that the service technician collects the check and returns it with the completed service order. To save extra work, instructions about the check and the rescheduled appointment time can be noted on a copy of the letter for the service technician.)

(Builder Logo)

(Date)

(New Homeowner)
(Address)

Dear (Homeowner's Name):

    Service order # _____ was issued on _____ for warranty work needed in your home.

    Several attempts to provide the work listed have been unsuccessful. Our commitment to fulfill the terms of your warranty requires that we pay you for the work indicated and permit you to schedule the needed repair at your convenience and with a repairperson of your choice.

    A check (# _____ based on the cost to (Builder's Company Name) for this work is enclosed. The service order will be voided and the item recorded as resolved in your file.

    if we can provide you with any information that will assist you in resolving this item on your own, please feel free to call me.

Sincerely,

(Signature)
Warranty Manager

cc: (Service technician or subcontractor)

off" a customer simply because the sub happens to dislike the customer.

Discretion and Confidentiality. Subs should refrain from commenting to homeowners about the work of other trades, even when asked to do so by the customer. It is often tempting for contractors to demonstrate their knowledge about many aspects of construction, evaluating the entire home and all the work in it. Expressing opinions about the quality of work or material supplied by another sub can be very damaging to all relationships involved. Once a customer hears from a technician that there is a "defect" in the home, nothing anyone else can say will dislodge that opinion. At times a sub may be able to provide a piece of technical information to resolve a customer's concern; but under no circumstances should the sub agree with or encourage the homeowner's negativity, regardless of the sub's personal opinion. Defending the sub's own work with comments such as "I know it's not right, but that's all the builder will pay for" is equally inappropriate and grounds for a builder to consider terminating the relationship. If a sub does notice any serious or potentially dangerous items, the sub should report them immediately to the builder for further inspection.

Criticizing the company, its products, or other employees, and revealing disagreements within the organization or between the builder and other subs also are inappropriate in discussions with homeowners. Internal workings of the company, including financial details the sub may be aware of or other pending business matters should not be discussed with homeowners. The builder usually will not want such tidbits to become general knowledge. Also, the customer may wonder what the gossipy sub will have to say about the customer's furniture, decorating, or personal business after leaving the home. Engaging in gossip is not part of the work assignment and is highly unprofessional.

Back Charges. Business sense and common sense can be compatible. Builders need not walk around all day searching for excuses to chip away at paychecks. Nickel-and-dime back charges can backfire when a builder needs help from a sub.

If an in-house service technician working in a home discovers and can repair a minor item that is technically the warranty responsibility of a sub, there is nothing wrong with having the technician proceed. The builder saves the administrative effort of issuing and tracking another service order, and the customer is saved the bother of another service appointment. Similarly, a wise sub occasionally will do a little something extra and not bill the builder for it. These are not major, expensive repair tasks; they are the petty, five- to twenty-five-dollar items that can drive everyone to distraction. A give-and-take, common sense approach is best and promotes a healthy team attitude that can save everyone a lot of hassle.

Good communication and mutual respect are integral to this system. Such thoughtful attention is wasted if it's all a secret. The parameters of who is willing to do what should be talked about informally, with examples tossed back and forth until everyone understands where the limits are. Two obvious limits are safety requirements and special technical knowledge. For example, a trained sub always should be called in to handle any gas line problems.

At some point, back charges will be necessary. A plumbing leak that results in drywall and hardwood floor damage means repair costs that the builder should not have to absorb. If the painter's ladder damages the kitchen vinyl, the painter, not the builder, should pay for the repair.

Alerting the sub to the facts surrounding the back charge and clearly explaining the amount involved is only fair. A telephone call followed by written notice (Figure 7-6), sent either in advance of or with the diminished check promotes open communication and can prevent conflicts. No one enjoys the surprise of opening a check and learning for the first time that $310.82 has been inexplicably deducted from the amount expected. Often, the subcontractor's business insurance may cover some of these charges and the sub will want to initiate the processing of such claims immediately.

Late Service Work

On occasion, every sub will be late completing a service order. Circumstances legitimately beyond the control of the subcontractor can prevent repairs from being performed. it is the sub's responsibility to let the builder know if access to the home is unavailable for some reason, or if a required part is back ordered. Usually, the builder then extends the deadline. When service work is continually late, however, everyone suffers. The homeowner is unhappy, the builder's reputation is damaged, and the relationship between the sub and the builder can be seriously strained.

Builders using an effective monitoring system can identify incomplete orders and intervene on behalf of the customer quickly and effectively. The sub should be aware of the tracking system and the penalties for failure to provide needed services.

Figure 7-6: Sample Subcontractor Notice

Subcontractor Notice

Date: _____

To: _____

_____

_____

☐ Our records show the following incomplete warranty work orders:

Community	Lot #	Homeowner	Work Order #	Date Issued
_____	_____	_____	_____	_____
_____	_____	_____	_____	_____
_____	_____	_____	_____	_____

Unless the work listed above is completed within five (5) days, payment of money due you may be delayed. If there is a reason for this delay in service, please advise us immediately.

☐ Payments are being delayed due to lack of response on the following overdue warranty work orders:

Community	Lot #	Homeowner	Work Order #	Date Issued
_____	_____	_____	_____	_____
_____	_____	_____	_____	_____
_____	_____	_____	_____	_____

Unless service is completed within five (5) days another contractor will perform the required work and the costs back charged to your company.

☐ It has been necessary to back charge your company as detailed below:

Community	Lot #	Homeowner	Work Order #	Date Issued
_____	_____	_____	_____	_____
_____	_____	_____	_____	_____

Amount: _____

Explanation:

_____

_____

If you have any questions regarding the above noted items, please call our office. We will be happy to discuss any details with you.

Sincerely,

(Builder)

Just as with back charges, quick communication regarding problems prevents disagreements and misunderstandings.

When work is late, the builder may make a friendly telephone call to remind the sub, send a written notice (Figure 7-6), or—in more serious cases—suspend payments or even hire someone else to perform the work and back charge the original sub. Termination is usually a last resort.

Special Situations

When a homeowner calls with an emergency (such as no heat), the builder also will use the telephone to relay the information to the heating contractor. To keep a good paper trail, a service order is still issued and the usual copies sent out. This can lead the heating contractor to call a homeowner for an appointment when the repair has already been completed. While the paper trail is needed, the duplication and confusion are not. By discussing emergency situations and agreeing on a method to handle them, everyone finds the process easier. In this example, the builder could write "Confirming Phone Call of December 12" on the service order. The note informs everyone that this is merely the paperwork catching up to the emergency, not a new problem.

Depending on the system the sub uses, a slight variation in normal procedures might expedite good service. If the sub has an office employee to track service work, an extra copy of the work order can support this additional enforcement. The sub who is in the field all the time may prefer that service orders be delivered to the construction trailer instead of being sent to an office through the mail.

Accommodating such individual needs when possible shows the builder's flexibility and willingness to support excellent service. A balance between flexibility and chaos must be maintained. The builder cannot function effectively when using a different system for each subcontractor.

The last item on the subcontractor's service agenda should be anything else the sub might want to discuss. After resolving any final issues or questions, these items should be written down so that any builder employee who is affected can be informed. For example, a plumber may wish to have a choice of who repairs drywall damage if a leak occurs. If the builder agrees to this, the warranty manager and accounting staff need to be made aware of the commitment. The key question here is, "Who else needs to know?"

By allowing subs a chance for input or questions, a builder encourages their involvement and commitment to service, thereby achieving one of the main objectives of the meeting.

Improving Existing Relationships

Unless procedural changes that apply to all subs (such as implementation of a computerized system) will be announced, group meetings between subs and the builder usually are unproductive, at least regarding service.

If one or more subcontractors are out of step with the rest of the team, the builder will see far better results from a one-on-one meeting than from a group pep talk. When the builder is angry or frustrated with a sub's service performance, a one-on-one meeting also provides a more effective forum to bring problems out in the open and resolve them.

Setting aside the assumption that the fault lies totally with the sub, the builder should schedule a calm, objective problem-solving session. The builder has three options: (1) solve the problems with the present sub, (2) replace the sub, or (3) continue putting up with unsatisfactory service. The last choice is unacceptable to a builder concerned about the company's reputation and future business. Repeated turnover of subcontractors is time-consuming and expensive. A builder and a veteran sub both have a big investment in their relationship. A sincere effort to improve communication first and service next is worth a try and will often resolve the problem.

The builder can prepare for such a meeting by reviewing the agenda used to orient new subs about service expectations, noting the areas that need improvement. Next, the builder can compile specific examples of poor service habits. The point is not to build a case against the sub in question, but to be able to provide concrete examples of what the builder sees as problem areas.

Keeping a Positive Tone

By approaching the meeting in a positive way, the builder can cover the major points without alienating the sub. To show good will, you can approach the discussion acknowledging some responsibility: "Perhaps we did not communicate our service expectations clearly enough . . . ." or "We've come to realize that as a company we must all provide better service and we need your help to do that." Another strategy to keep the discussion positive is to express a belief that things will work out: "I'm sure we'll be able to come to an understanding on this. . . ."

To be fair, the builder should give the sub an opportunity to explain possible misunderstandings and also to mention parts of the builder's system that may impede good service from this sub. Communication between the builder and sub may need some fine-tuning. This type of discussion can lead to minor variations in the system or even major improvements for the builder and all subs. When working with twenty to thirty subcontractors, some flexibility will bring better results than a rigid or arbitrary attitude.

Enforcing Policies

Builders are mainly concerned with three elements of a sub's service performance: the timing, the attitude, and the quality of repair work. Of these, the timing is the easiest to track and ironically the one most often violated. Improving service usually involves six steps:

- making an honest assessment of current performance,
- setting realistic goal(s),
- developing a plan and supporting system to achieve the goal(s),
- monitoring changes indicated by results,
- making changes indicated by results, and
- repeating the above steps until everyone is happy and rich (caution: this may take a long time).

The best intentions to improve service will fail to achieve anything noteworthy if the later steps are not performed with the same zeal as the initial steps. Follow-through is the part of the process that demands dedicated focus and long-term commitment from management.

Monitoring Performance. Any reporting system should be designed to measure precisely what *needs* to be measured. Elaborate computer systems can produce pages and pages of reports that reconfigure the same information many different—and sometimes important—ways. No mortal can possibly review and digest all of them, not even a builder.

To learn how long it takes each sub to complete service orders, the builder needs a straightforward tracking system (see chapter 6). If no tracking has been done in the past, simply developing a useful picture from this information will cause sufficient stress for several months: fancier reports can be added later, once the critical element is under control.

Each sub should receive performance feedback with a builder evaluation (see Figure 7-7). Kudos to subs are just as important as reprimands. Some will be surprised. Some will present a callous "So what's it to ya?" attitude; these sometimes turn out to be the subs who show the greatest improvement. But all of the subs will know a new era has begun for their service performance.

Many builders have obtained significant improvements by circulating a summary (Figure 7-8) rating the performance of all subs. The subs gain a perspective on where they stand relative to

---

Figure 7-7: Sample Report Cards

Good Service

(Builder Logo)

September 12, 199X

(Subcontractor's Name)
(Address)

RE: Warranty service, month of August, 199X

Dear (Contact Name):

A routine review of service records shows the following service orders were issued to your company in the month of August:

Service order #	Complete	Incomplete	Comment
2457	x		
2468	x		
2490	x		
2551	x		
2572		x	HO out of town til 9/15
2574	x		

Please compare this information to your records and notify us of any discrepancies.

Thank you for your cooperation in completing the work listed. Your continued support contributes to our mutual business success and we appreciate your efforts in providing our home buyers with exceptional service.

Sincerely,

(Signature)
Warranty Manager

cc: Purchasing

(continued on next page)

Figure 7-7, continued

Poor Service

(Builder Logo)

September 13, 199X

(Subcontractor's Name)
(Address)

RE: Warranty service, month of August, 199X

Dear (Contact Name):

A routine review of service records shows the following service orders were issued to your company in the month of August:

Service order #	Complete	Incomplete	Comment
2455		x	Parts on order
2482		x	Parts on order
2501	x		
2530		x	Parts on order
2558		x	No response
2577	x		(To be reinspected)
2593		x	No response

Please compare this information to your records and notify us of any discrepancies.

It is our intention to work with contractors who share a strong belief in providing our home buyers with exceptional service. We believe that by calling your attention to these outstanding items immediate improvement in service will occur. Under those circumstances, we look forward to continuing to work with your company.

Sincerely,

(Signature)
Warranty Manager

cc: Purchasing

their peers. Those who do well strive to maintain that level, while those who do not feel very uncomfortable. By alerting subs in advance that such feedback will begin on a certain date, everyone has a chance to improve before the first summary is released.

The builder should think carefully before deciding to make tracking information generally available to subs. For one thing, the builder's staff will be expected to perform at the same (or superior) levels. Also, consistent failure of subs to meet required

Figure 7-8: Summary Report, Subcontractor Performance

More elaborate reports are possible, but the main message of this summary is to remind subcontractors that someone is watching their performance. A simple report is adequate to accomplish that purpose.

DATE: September 13, 199X
TO: (each subcontractor listed)
FROM: (Name), Warranty Manager
RE: Service Order Completions, Month of August

Subcontractor	Service orders issued	On-time completions	
Hot Air, Cold Air	9	9	100%
Pipes, Inc.	10*	9	90%
Volts Electric	7	7	100%
Brush Painting	19	17	89%
Straight Walls Drywall	8	6	75%
Hi Class Cabinets	14	4	29%
Open Windows, Inc.	13	9	69%
Pretty Floors and Counters	12	9	75%
Rainy Roof	3	3	100%
Gray Concrete, Inc.	5**	3	60%

Notes:
 *One homeowner out of town until 9/15.
**Outstanding items pending grade corrections by construction department.

ALSO: We are happy to welcome "Shiney Drawers, Inc." as the cabinet company for our upcoming 94-home community at Happy Meadows. We look forward to adding your 100% to this list!

cc: Shiney Drawers, Inc.

response times *must* result in some action on the part of the builder. Once revealed, problems must be addressed: the builder will feel a pressure to reprimand or replace subs who perform below standard. The builder who fails to do this sends a dangerous message: "See, we know these subs are slow but we are letting them get away with it." Similarly, when the builder replaces a sub whose poor performance has failed to improve after several months, this action also sends a clear message. Once a reporting system is set up and the results circulated, the builder is committed to take action. Allowing the reporting system to operate for a couple of months before making the results general knowledge allows the builder to evaluate results and prepare an appropriate response.

As with other aspects of service work, common sense should temper policy. If the concrete contractor has eleven outstanding service orders but there are eighteen inches of snow on the ground, that sub's work may not be completed within the designated time frame. Service orders for exterior paint work are also subject to weather conditions. Such jobs can be "excused" from tracking or placed on hold during the months when inclement weather is a legitimate factor.

Quality of work can be difficult to monitor. If each time a builder hears a homeowner's complaint or compliment about a sub's work or attitude, the incident is noted and added to the service file for the sub involved, specific details will be readily available when builder and sub sit down to review service performance. If the complaint has to do with quality of the work, the builder should inspect the work and note an evaluation in the file. In this way, criticisms from homeowners about work that the builder determines to be within standards will not be held against the subcontractor.

Having experienced the sales process with the homeowner, the builder is in a good position to temper a customer's comments. Some customers will not be satisfied with the attitude or workmanship of anyone; no sub should be blamed for failing to please such individuals. At the other extreme, a subcontractor file containing complaints from almost every homeowner indicates that a serious talk is long overdue.

Homeowner surveys, postcard questionnaires enclosed with service orders, or comments generated by customer focus groups all offer valid additional input on the quality of service and treatment homeowners receive. The builder should review information from all of these sources before making final selections of subs when bids are received on new work.

When Trouble Occurs. Sooner or later, a customer-subcontractor interaction will produce a chemistry so negative that any further communication between the two will cause more harm than good. In severe cases, the homeowner may flatly state that he or she will not let the sub in the home again.

While the builder could insist that work will not be done at all unless by the assigned sub, this approach is not conducive to high quality service. Worse, if the sub involved actually earned the homeowner's low opinion, such a stance can damage the customer's opinion of the builder. Even after hearing from both sides, the builder may not really know who is at fault in such situations. In fact, knowing who is at fault does not solve the immediate problem, anyway. The question is, what can be done?

First the builder must discover exactly what is wrong. If the homeowner is displeased with an individual from the company but someone else can be sent to handle service calls, the problem is relatively easy to solve. If the complaint is more general and the customer refuses all contact with the subcontractor's organization, stronger measures may be needed.

Another aspect to consider is what work is left to be done and how much time remains on the warranty? If the complaint pertains to a year-end service visit, the work was completed and the homeowner has only three days of warranty coverage remaining, no steps may need to be taken. However, if an altercation occurs early in the warranty period or in the middle of a major repair, the builder may prefer to arrange for completion by an alternate subcontractor. A simple and straightforward letter of agreement can establish the details of the change and provide the customer with peace of mind. It is critically important to provide the exact dates on which the alternate sub will replace the original, at the expense of the offending subcontractor. The first sub should be informed of any work ordered to be performed by the replacement. The customer needs to know the replacement's name and telephone number, particularly if the repair involves one of the three critical subs—heat, plumbing, or electrical.

When to Replace a Subcontractor

Some builders seem to enjoy firing subcontractors. While repeated firings may be exciting, ultimately the effect is confusion and finger-pointing. No one is ever certain who did which job, what the status of installation or repair work really is, or whom to call in a legitimate emergency. Replacing subs frequently produces very little improvement in service.

Even a highly service-oriented replacement sub will be unfamiliar with the builder's particular system, or lack parts standard for someone else's equipment. The new sub also may not know where streets are, and will be unaware of which homeowners are fuss-budgets and which are never on time for their appointments. Understandable delays and mix-ups can ensue. It can take many time-consuming conversations to get the newcomer aligned with the builder's system. During this time, service quality is at best static, More often it is diminished, at least temporarily.

It is far better to hire subcontractors with great care, orient them in detail, monitor their work faithfully, and provide regular feedback for improvement. When specific problems arise, they must be brought to the sub's attention and calmly discussed. Clear input from the builder on exactly what needs to change often brings the desired improvement.

When attempts to gain the cooperation of the sub have failed to produce any improvement, repetition of identified problems can be a sign that no sincere effort is being made to correct them. Still, the decision to replace a sub involves weighing many factors.

The builder must answer five basic questions: What is worse for overall service performance, breaking in a new sub or continuing to work with this one? How is the sub's performance in other areas of the relationship: technical skills, adherence to construction schedules, and pricing? How many homes are involved in the complaint? It makes little sense to change subs for the last two houses in a subdivision of 116 homes. Is low price in the present going to damage sales in the future? And finally, does everyone in the organization feel the sub should be replaced, but inertia, fear of change or lack of time have delayed the decision to do so? The energy drain that results from enduring a sub whose performance is poor is significant and should not be tolerated. Further, word soon gets around among other subs that the builder accepts poor performance. This reputation can result in other subs putting forth less effort, and a downward spiral begins.

When a Sub Disappears. Sometimes a subcontractor simply becomes unavailable. Relocation, bankruptcy, retirement, even death—whatever factors cause a sub to become unavailable, some basics need to be considered in developing a plan to handle the results. The builder can evaluate the effects of this situation by considering the following questions:

- How many homeowners are affected?
- How many warranty months remain for each of the affected homeowners (see chapter 10)?
- What has been the rate of call backs for this sub?
- How many warranty service orders are currently outstanding?
- What resources are available (in other words, how much money does the builder currently owe the subcontractor)?
- Will any former employees of the sub continue the business? If so, are they acceptable candidates to complete the work?

The homeowners for whom the departing sub was responsible deserve comparable service. The builder cannot say, "Well, 'Hot Air' went out of business, so you'll just have to take care of your furnace problem on your own." The builder's warranty obligation to the homeowner does not disappear because a sub does.

In cases involving bankruptcy, subcontractors' personal integrity may require that they meet their obligations regardless of their financial struggles. However, the best intentions will not produce results if available resources do not support the effort. The builder may use money that is owed to the sub to help provide services to the homeowners, back charging the work of another company against the balance until it is gone (or until a bankruptcy court demands it). Once this fund is used, however, further service comes out of the builder's pocket.

If a sub decides to retire, the builder usually will have enough notice to phase in a new sub and phase out the former one. Careful records need to be kept of which sub is responsible for which home. At some point, the replacement may take over warranty service on all remaining homes to free the outgoing sub completely. This can be a service that is paid for on a call-by-call basis or as a flat rate negotiated between the builder and the two subs.

When firing a sub, the builder obviously has more control and usually some advance knowledge. The builder can prepare a plan, and determine a percentage of payment to be retained from money due the sub based on historic performance and the number of months of warranty coverage remaining on affected homes.

When a subcontractor dies, the homeowners affected will certainly feel sorry about the event, but they will nonetheless expect warranty service to continue. Service continues, arranged for from another contractor. When the funds owed to the former sub are depleted, needed payments will come out of the builder's pocket.

When a subcontractor is no longer available, regardless of the circumstances, the basic issue is what arrangements the builder can make to continue providing services. In the end, the builder may pay all or part of the bill. The risk inherent in having a warranty commitment to customers should be kept in mind when discussing service with incoming subs; it can become a very significant factor in the builder's business plan.

Builder Obligations to Subs

After a typical Monday that includes phone calls from three customers registering complaints about subs, a builder can find it challenging to maintain a balanced attitude. However, it helps to remember the other eighty-six service orders issued this month that were completed successfully by the same group of subs.

A healthy builder's perspective will include seeing warranty service from the sub's side. Consider the procedures and standards. Are they fair and reasonable? Are they applied consistently, but not inflexibly? Is there room for common sense and logic? Are subs protected from unrealistic demands from customers? In most cases, a sub has no chance to screen the home buyers. Subs should have the opportunity to review the standards and commitments made to the customer regarding each trade. This offers them a chance to help with adjusting customer expectations. Subcontractors often contribute technical information that is of real use in educating customers.

Respect the value of the subcontractors' time. Sending the sub to the wrong house, providing inaccurate telephone numbers, or providing incomplete information about the requested work causes frustration and needless delays.

Recognize that at least two sides exist for every story. Asking to hear the sub's version is always fair, and can save the builder the embarrassment of having to apologize for making accusations before hearing all the facts.

Finally, keep in mind the value of a compliment for a job well done. The unexciting but consistently dependable sub deserves (and needs) a thank-you as much as the one who makes dramatic and flamboyant efforts. Feedback to subs should not be limited to criticism, but should include expressions of appreciation when appropriate. These might include simple gestures such as taking someone to lunch, a phone call just to say "thank you" for a particular task, a letter to the sub's owner praising an exceptional service technician, or recognition in the builder's newsletter. Forwarding a copy of any written notes of appreciation received from homeowners is a must; many companies display these on bulletin boards. More elaborate demonstrations involving certificates of appreciation, gifts, and awards are possible as well. Nothing can take the place of routinely saying, "Thanks, we appreciate all you've done."

Requesting feedback from subcontractors on an annual survey (Figure 7-9) can bring interesting results. The builder's interest in their opinions will surprise and please many subs.

Every time a customer has contact with a subcontractor something is contributed to the overall impression that customer has of the builder. The builder's reputation may be only as good as that of the worst sub. Establishing good service practice from well-oriented subs is tremendously challenging but essential to a successful service program.

Figure 7-9: Sample Subcontractor Survey

Subcontractor Survey

We'd like to ask your opinion . . .

We are sincerely interested in your comments regarding both our product and service. Please take a few minutes to complete the questions below and return this sheet in the enclosed stamped, preaddressed envelope.

yes no 1) Are the construction standards and specs you are expected to meet clear and complete?

yes no 2) Are these standards and specs consistently and fairly enforced?

yes no 3) Is adequate notice provided regarding routine scheduling of your work?

yes no 4) Is adequate notice provided regarding customer-approved changes from normal plans?

yes no 5) Are our homes ready for your work when you arrive on the job?

yes no 6) Are cleanup procedures clear and enforced?

yes no 7) Are safe practices in place and enforced?

yes no 8) Do customers interfere with the progress of your efforts?

yes no 9) Is supervision adequate, allowing you an opportunity to ask questions and obtain quick and accurate answers?

yes no 10) Are your invoices/draws processed efficiently and payments made on time?

yes no 11) Are warranty standards and procedures clear and fairly enforced?

yes no 12) Is there anything we can do to assist you in providing better service to our customers?

_____

_____

Please add any other comments our company, methods, product, personnel, or service; include any suggestions you have to save time, money, effort, or improve our product.

_____

_____

_____

Thank You! Your feedback is most valuable to us in improving our product and service.

8

SURVIVING CONFLICT WITH CUSTOMERS

Regardless of the best efforts, customer conflict will occur in every business. Homebuilding and remodeling businesses are certainly not exceptions.

Conflict about warranty issues need not destroy the builder's relationship with a customer. Disagreements can be minor or major, but how the builder responds to those conflicts will determine the amount of damage they do to the company's relationship with the customer and the builder's overall image. Angry customers are likely to talk about their experience to anyone who will listen. Generally, an angry customer can be expected to speak about a problem with nine to thirteen people; but the average person has about two hundred-fifty acquaintances. The builder may be 100 percent right—but the customer will probably not mention that when repeating the story, whether to one person or two hundred.

By responding to conflict constructively and professionally, the builder can minimize the damage and maximize the chances of regaining customers' trust and respect. Learning from experience, builders can reduce the chances of future conflicts and improve their skills in responding when such problems do occur.

Points of Conflict

Conflict with a customer can arise over a wide variety of things. Generally for a builder or remodeler, warranty disagreements relate to one of the following items: the purchase and sales agreement, builder policy, standards, the builder's personality, or external factors.

Purchase and Sales Agreement

Confrontations can occur over change orders or selections, disputes over timing, pricing, inclusions, standard or optional items, or even what is going in the vacant lot across the street. If the home is in warranty, chances are good any early disputes have been settled; however, a customer's positive opinion is not guaranteed simply because the home is occupied. While the warranty staff usually is uninvolved in early issues, residual negative emotions may affect their dealings with the customer.

Policy or Procedure

Disagreements can develop over methods and procedures. For example, friction may occur over the fact that payment is required before implementing a change order, or that warranty items must be submitted in writing.

Standards

If the customer's personal standard is different from the industry standard, he or she may try to get the builder to adhere to that personal standard. During warranty, conflict frequently arises over the choice of a method of repair, and customers often demand complete replacement rather than repair.

Personality and Professionalism

A missed appointment, a technician's rudeness, an uncaring attitude, or a builder employee's lack of patience are just a few things that can alienate a homeowner. Careful hiring and training of all staff who are in contact with customers helps develop a professional atmosphere and minimize the likelihood of this kind of conflict. Some conflicts result from a buildup of minor problems and frustrations. Although the specific incident that triggers a customer complaint may be very minor, the customer's anger can be impressive. A customer who feels disappointed, cheated, or taken advantage of cannot feel good about doing business with the builder. When handling such situations, a builder's attitude can be key to easing—or aggravating—the tension.

External Factors

If the mortgage company, movers, job insecurity, marital or family problems, or health concerns have upset the homeowner, the negative emotions can affect how the customer approaches warranty personnel. Few customers will preface a verbal attack by explaining, "I'm sorry I'm going to scream at you, but my son just failed ninth grade and I can't stand my new boss. I feel like taking it out on someone, and you happened along."

Responding to Conflict

Builders must recognize that they cannot control other people. Builders can control only their own thoughts, feelings, and actions. (Some days, they will seem to have only marginal success controlling those.) Unable to prevent, or even completely predict confrontation, the builder had best learn how to cope with it.

By disciplining themselves to avoid defensiveness and remain objective, builders' reps can often salvage a relationship and the customer's goodwill. The warranty period comes at the end of a long process of customer and builder interaction. All that has gone before, good or bad, has influenced the attitude of the customer. This attitude, in turn, affects how service personnel respond—especially if the customer is belligerent and service personnel have no clue as to why. When approached by a hostile customer, warranty staff must avoid the natural tendency to become defensive. Keeping the long-term nature of this relationship in mind helps: the warranty rep can help ensure that the relationship settles down and begins to function smoothly. Even if the effort is only partially successful, adept handling of conflict can minimize negative word-of-mouth advertising. Developing a collection of conflict-resolution techniques will pay off.

Recognizing Conflict

Consciously recognizing a confrontation puts the warranty rep mentally on the alert. Customers do not call at 9:00 a.m. and announce, "I'm going to call back at 2:00 this afternoon and be angry—get ready." Neither does the builder schedule the confrontation. Warranty personnel do not wake up in the morning and say to themselves, "I can't wait to get to the office and ruin the day for some homeowner!" When conflict strikes, no one has time to sit calmly and ponder how to respond; the problem must be addressed right away.

Often, disagreements develop gradually in the course of a conversation that began normally. Sometimes conflict develops over several conversations. It is all too easy to go from normal conversation to aggravated conversation to screaming. Warranty reps must be sensitive to such tendencies and respond quickly if the communication begins to get out of control. The sooner a disagreement is recognized, the sooner conflict-handling techniques can be applied.

It helps to identify not only the general fact that a conflict is developing, but also the nature of the disagreement: Does the problem involve the contract? Is it a matter of policy or procedure? Is there disagreement over standards? Has someone's behavior or personality led to the customer complaint? If a combination of items has caused the customer's anger, each issue will need to be resolved one at a time.

Practicing Self Control

An angry person can be irrational while the emotions flow unencumbered by self-control. Getting drawn into the anger results in two irrational people, both trying to prove they are right. Chances of a successful outcome evaporate when this occurs. Arguing does not convince anyone of anything. It only causes more damage to an already injured relationship. New information, new insight, logic, or calm repetition of the facts may change someone's mind once he or she calms down enough to hear the information. Losing control and screaming back will not. Using the following tips may help builders to avoid getting caught up in angry emotion.

Remember, Anger is Energy. Most people cannot remain angry to the point of yelling and screaming for more than a few minutes. Being that angry is an exhausting activity. Keeping this in mind makes it easier to wait for the anger to subside without getting caught in it.

Stay Seated. When a person is in a standing position, the "flight or fight" stress response is more likely to take over. Efforts to maintain self-control are physically more likely to be successful if a person remains seated.

Maintain Normal Conversational Volume. Responding to an enraged person in reasonable tones reinforces the calmer speaker's control. Sometimes, maintaining or even lowering one's tone of voice will itself defuse a customer's anger, helping the person relax so that a more normal discussion can resume.

Allow Disagreement. Saying, "I regret the company is having a disagreement with you," is a straightforward way to refer to an issue. Naming a conflict makes it seem more controllable for both the customer and the builder. This technique signals empathy for the customer without implying argument.

Use Time Outs. If control begins to slip away, it can help to take a *time out*. The service rep can suggest, "Ms. Jones, you have me at a disadvantage. Let me pull your file and review it. I'll call you back in ten minutes"; or "I can see that we need to discuss this in more detail to get it straightened out. Unfortunately, someone is waiting to see me. May I call you back in fifteen minutes when we'll be able to talk without interruption?" The short break allows the customer to calm down and allows the employee to check for any information needed to respond. A few quiet minutes to think may produce the perfect solution. (Caution: When using this technique, it is *imperative* to call back within the promised time. Failing to do so may further irritate the customer, escalating the situation.)

Swap Reps. This technique should be used rarely. Occasionally, a strong personality conflict between two people needs to be recognized. A volatile customer-builder rep combination whose every conversation deteriorates into an argument contributes nothing to customer satisfaction or a builder's reputation. It is better for the customer, the company, and the warranty rep if someone else handles that particular customer. Another advantage to this approach is that the new rep can prepare by reviewing past problems. The new rep sometimes can respond better because the problems are not a surprise.

Listen Actively. The time to plan an answer is not while the customer is talking. To respond properly, a rep must truly hear the other person's words and the message between the words. To eliminate any confusions it can help to repeat the events or facts back to the customer.

Customer anger often can be traced to the feeling that no one in the builder's office understands or will take the time to listen to the customer's point of view. Showing the customer that the message has been received in full detail and with every implication relieves a lot of this frustration.

Take Notes. Service representatives should take notes and be sure the customer knows they are doing so. As with repeating details back over the telephone, this demonstrates that the customer is being taken seriously. Every customer feels each issue is special. People are more convinced that a resolution is possible if they realize their concerns are being heard.

Ask Questions. As much as possible, reps should use "what" questions instead of "why" questions. For example, asking, "Why wasn't our service satisfactory?" invites antagonistic answers along the lines of, "Why? Maybe your manager is incompetent! How should I know why you can't do things right?"

The customer does not know—or care—*why*. The customer knows *what:* What happened. What did not happen. "What was it about our service that disappointed you?" is more likely to bring a factual response: "The service technician was 20 minutes late, and then didn't have the necessary parts. And then I discovered your repair person had chipped the wood. Now we've got another problem to fix!" This response gives the rep a place to begin in resolving the issue. Figure 8-1 presents suggested responses to some classic attacks.

Looking for Solutions

After an initial flood of vehemence, a customer may request a very reasonable action. Then again, the customer may not. But if warranty reps fail to give customers a chance to say what they want, a quick and comfortable solution may be overlooked.

In almost every case, regardless of the specific conflict, one key issue needs to be settled before the builder can effectively respond to the customer: Is the conflict the builder's fault? The reflex to defend the builder no matter what is not conducive to good customer relations. A customer can spot an excuse, lie, cover-up or runaround before the sentence is half finished. Is this a situation where the builder has failed to meet certain commitments? Were commitments honored, but the customer is unhappy with the result? Recognizing the difference can be difficult, especially when dealing with an emotional customer. Even more confusing are situations that fall somewhere in-between.

Failed Commitments. If the customer is angry because the builder has not met contractual commitments and obligations, the correction usually becomes obvious once the problem is recognized. Specific warranty conflicts usually have specific responses. If a service order is overdue, the builder's action clearly should include apologizing to the customer and contacting the sub. If a repaired item broke again the next day, additional work clearly is in order. If the customer complains about the quality of the work performed, the builder should inspect the repair work.

If a builder has not met promised levels of service, the customer's anger may be appropriate. A fair hearing, acknowledgment, and apology may be all that the customer seeks. Following through on appropriate corrections should reestablish good relations.

Figure 8-1: Classic Attacks

Classic attacks are the threats that homeowners sometimes make when they have run out of other arguments. Unfortunately, there will always be those few people who make unreasonable demands. While some flexibility is good, giving in to customers' scare tactics quickly can become dangerously expensive. The correct response to such aggression is to (1) stay calm, (2) stay rational, (3) express confidence, not fear. The customer's agenda is to scare the builder or builder rep into doing what the customer wants. Often, the tone of a builder's reaction is more important than the actual words spoken.

The builder's goal is to reestablish good relations regardless of what's causing the disagreement—and the best chance of accomplishing this is to refuse to get angry or become defensive. The builder should operate from the perspective that such persons believe they deserve what they are requesting.

One way to prepare for this kind of conflict is to role-play. Rehearsing allows staff to anticipate potential problems, and to feel more confident that they are ready with responses. Some classic attacks are presented below, along with possible responses.

ATTACK # 1:   I used to be in the construction business. . . .

ATTACK STRATEGY: To intimidate the warranty rep by implying that the caller has knowledge about the industry and therefore can challenge the builder's policies or procedures with authority.

RESPONSE: Then I know you understand how difficult it is to anticipate the choices your buyers would want you to make. I'm sure you remember choosing between subcontractor A and subcontractor B, product A and product B. . . . Each choice plugs a number into the price. When you're finished, you total the numbers and there's your selling price. I regret that we made a choice or two that you would have made differently if you had been building the house. I hope you remember when you were looking at several builders that we came closer to matching your choices than the others you considered. Otherwise, you wouldn't have bought your home from us. Most people don't have the perspective you have. I really regret that we made a choice you disagree with in planning your home; I am glad you understand how that can happen.

ATTACK # 2:   I paid $X for this house. . . .

ATTACK STRATEGY: What is left unsaid at the end of this statement is "and my expectations have not been met." This hidden judgment is therefore the one that the builder must address.

RESPONSE: Even if your home had only cost half what it did, we would still want you to be happy with it. Our commitment was to deliver a home at the quality level we show in our models, and then live up to the standards we provided you with for the warranty. The kind of people we sell to have very high personal standards; we work hard to meet those whenever possible.

ATTACK # 3:   This isn't built according to code. . . .

ATTACK STRATEGY: The not-so-hidden threat here is "Unless you do what I want, I'm going to get you in trouble with the building department." Often, the builder can counter this kind of direct pressure by defusing the anger behind it—instead of resisting the complaint outright, first find a point on which builder and customer can to agree, and go from there.

RESPONSE: Code violations are unacceptable to us also. We have each of our houses inspected at several points during construction, but building inspectors aren't perfect, either. If one of our homes does have a code violation, we will correct it. I'm not aware of the specific code you are making reference to, however. If you would forward a copy of it to me with your written notice, we'll set up another inspection and order any necessary corrections immediately.

(continued on next page)

(continued from previous page)

ATTACK # 4:   I want to talk to (owner, president . . .)!

ATTACK STRATEGY: Many people think if they can cut through to the person at the top—bypassing standard procedures—they can also bypass policy, or at least persuade an authority to bend the rules for them. This attack also plays on employees' fears that customer complaints to a boss might get them fired. Usually, however, the owner (president, or CEO) has established the very policies the builder rep is defending—and will stand by them, for good reason.

RESPONSE: I regret you feel that's necessary. Mr. X's extension is 200, and his secretary's name is Bob. Mr. X does travel a lot and may be out of town, but he will return your call. Before you take your time in trying to reach him, there is one more point I'd like you to be aware of. I'm not making up these standards and policies as I go along. I am applying the standards and policies Mr. X gave me to follow. However, if you believe you can convince him to make a change in them, please feel free to contact him.

ATTACK # 5:   I've already talked to my attorney. . . .

ATTACK STRATEGY: Here the strategy is pure intimidation. If the caller is not bluffing, there truthfully is not much the warranty rep can do to resolve the situation on the telephone. The warranty rep's goal should therefore be calmly gather and record any pertinent information about the situation, in case it will be needed later by the company lawyer. If the customer is bluffing, the warranty rep's refusal to be "ruffled" by the threat may of itself bring the conversation back to a reasonable discussion.

RESPONSE # 1:   I regret that we're having this disagreement. But you must do what you feel you have to do.

RESPONSE # 2:   I regret that we're having this disagreement. I hope that before you speak to your attorney he or she has copies of your contract and warranty information so that your attorney has access to all the same information that I am looking at.

RESPONSE # 3:   I regret that we're having this disagreement. If it will help to get this matter resolved, I'll be happy to talk with your attorney. Perhaps I can call him? (Note: A formal letter from a customer's attorney is quite another matter from this time-honored threat. When genuine legal action is possible, builders should contact their personal or company attorneys.)

All these scenarios presuppose that the contract has been satisfied, and that all warranty standards have been met. If the customer's complaint is valid and something is not right, however, the correct response is to apologize and take care of the problem as quickly as possible.

Warranty representatives can begin immediately to reestablish trust by making and keeping an interim promise. For example, the rep can promise to call back within a certain time frame with some additional information or an update.

Again, it is imperative to tell the truth. Promising actions that cannot be delivered is foolish. Suppose the customer requests that a problem be corrected within 24 hours and the builder knows that simply will not happen. Saying "we'll try," knowing there is no chance of succeeding, makes everything worse. Solving an immediate problem by creating a bigger long-term one does not make sense. Trust is built on honesty, not on agreement. Saying, "I know this is not the answer you want to hear, but I also want you to know you can trust what I tell you," will gain the respect of many customers.

Managing Failed Expectations. If the conflict is over a warranty denial and the customer still feels the repair should be supplied, a careful review of all the facts is in order. Usually, the customer sincerely believes he or she deserves the service. The rep should try to understand why the customer feels that way. In reviewing the facts, the builder may discover something previously overlooked and decide that the customer has a valid point.

When an objective review determines that the company has met all obligations, warranty reps can focus on what, if anything, can be done. When the customer says, "I want a new driveway with no cracks in it," the rep can offer, "Your warranty provides that we will caulk cracks in concrete flatwork. A new drive would most likely develop new cracks."

Even if the ultimate answer is still no, most customers will appreciate a builder's willingness to reconsider and explain further. Involving an impartial, expert third party may help to settle the matter. Additional technical information provided by someone uninvolved with the repair bill often carries more credibility.

Giving in to customers' excessive demands just to keep them happy is a mistake. Providing one $200 "extra" repair will be only the beginning. Soon comes a request for another small repair, and then another. The customer tells a neighbor, who now begins to expect similar, favored service. Then the builder discovers how much has been spent trying to keep one person happy. Ultimately, the builder begins to feel taken advantage of and eventually refuses further favors. The conflict that occurs at this point is the *same* conflict that would have occurred before the extra services were supplied.

Customers who make excessive demands will continue to make them until they learn the builder will not give in. Not every customer will play by the builder's rules, even when made fully aware of them. If the builder has faith in the company's standards and has honestly met them, the builder can feel justified in enforcing those standards.

Sometimes customers have a hidden agenda. Extreme reactions often indicate a hidden agenda. If the Joneses hysterically demand an entirely new vinyl floor because of a tiny chip in the surface, chances are excellent somewhere in the conversation they will casually say, "Since you're replacing it anyway, we'd want to pick a different color." If the warranty standards are clearly written, they will specify that patching is an acceptable repair. The customer already will have agreed to these terms. Whether a builder decides to give in to such hidden agendas is a matter of individual builder philosophy. Such decisions should be made on a case-by-case basis and balanced against the implications for the customer's neighbors. The builder must consider what kind of precedent is being set. It may be better in the long run to risk a conflict now with the Joneses than to risk one later with each of their six neighbors. Nothing is wrong with doing something extra for a customer as long as the builder is fully aware if the risks inherent in the action. Often it is better (and simpler) to remain firm on stated standards.

Obscure Procedures. When the disagreement pertains to a policy or procedure, builder employees should beware of applying policies unthinkingly. Warranty reps should compare the normal procedures with what the customer wants. Do circumstances justify making an exception to normal policy? Well-trained warranty reps will be able to make responsible judgment calls when necessary. If the builder is convinced that normal policy should still apply, explaining the reasons behind that conclusion may also convince the homeowner.

Countering Drastic Tactics

Today's consumer does not lack imagination. When disappointed by a builder, homeowners can find many ways to make their unhappiness apparent. As a general rule, a reputable builder will survive such attacks unscathed. The secret is to stay calm, maintain a sense of humor, and keep an open door to communications with the offended customer.

Pickets, Signs in the Yard. One version of sales-office "blackmail" that some customers employ is picketing the model center or installing a "Before you buy here, talk to me" sign in the front yard of their home. One clever sales manager responded by setting up refreshments for her picketers. The excitement brought increased traffic and she sold two homes that weekend. Another sales manager took a photograph of a front yard sign and sent it to the homeowner with the note, "When you put your home on the market, I'll share this with area realtors." The sign was down the next day.

Builders must always weigh their principles against their worry that such antagonistic activities will hurt business. Keeping in mind that giving in too easily will only show this customer that aggressive complaints are effective, a builder may decide to stand firm. A well-written letter from an attorney often puts a quick end to such activities.

The Community Instigator. Almost every subdivision has an instigator—someone who feels compelled to organize all the homeowners into a cohesive force in order to get what they want from the builder. In many cases, some legitimate reasons for unrest may exist. Once formed, such vigilante groups can do real harm to a builder's reputation, whether or not the uproar is deserved. By fulfilling all commitments and meeting stated standards, by listening and responding quickly when a customer complains, the builder can effectively remove the audience an instigator requires to perform. It is best to deal with members of vigilante groups one at a time. In group meetings, individual frustrations can combine, encouraging the group's anger and creating an impossible situation for the builder.

Consumer Protection Agencies. The first time a builder gets a letter from the Better Business Bureau, he or she will most likely be both angered and hurt. There is no need for either emotion. The BBB and other similar agencies serve a necessary function. When a consumer files a complaint with them, they must respond by checking out the complaint. Becoming angry with agency people only distracts the builder from finding out the cause of—and the solution for—the problem.

The builder who has been fair and honest has nothing to hide. As with the media, an open willingness to communicate often forestalls any suspicion that the customer is justified in the complaint. Responding with a calm summary of facts and events will usually convince consumer protection staff that the customer's complaint is either unfounded or exaggerated. Of course, if the customer's request was justified and reasonable, the builder should follow through with the repair.

Media. A telephone call from a reporter can raise a builder's blood pressure even faster than a letter from the Better Business Bureau. Nonetheless, the same calm response is appropriate. Demonstrating a willingness to answer questions with factual information rather than with an emotional retaliation goes a long way to establishing the builder's integrity in the reporter's mind.

Threats of Legal Action. Small claims court has become a more frequently exercised option for customers. Increased limits on the claims allowed make this exercise worth the modest filing fee and the time involved.

When notified that a small claims case against the company is pending, the builder should review the history of the relationship with the customer and the specific complaint. If the customer's claim has any validity, the builder should provide the requested repair. If not, the builder should prepare to present the company's side of the story in court.

A complete and accurate file, with records documenting all communications with the customer, will be invaluable. (This is when all that filing suddenly makes sense.) Copies of all relevant records should be made prior to the hearing, as the court may retain—at least for a period of time—all the original documents. The builder should go to court prepared to spend the entire day. The docket will list the cases to be heard and in what order, but no one can predict how long each case will take, so the builder may be in for a wait.

When called upon, the builder presents the company's side of the story. The homeowner will do the same, and the court will render a decision. No one can predict what will happen in small claims court any more than any other court. The best defense against being taken to court is to conduct business in such a way that customers do not feel they have any justifiable claim. Failing that, good files are the next best thing.

Even if the builder's written warranty includes a clause setting forth a formal dispute resolution procedure such as arbitration, lawsuits are always possible. When seriously threatened with a lawsuit, the builder's best course is assistance from the builder's personal or company attorney. Some builders may be tempted to "save" money by representing themselves in court—however, in a courtroom setting the builder may say exactly the wrong thing to a customer's attorney. This situation can be disastrous. When a customer gets an attorney, a builder's best protection is to get one, too.

Formal Dispute Resolution

When good relations with a customer remain elusive despite sincere efforts, having a formal method of dispute resolution as a part of the system can be an important safety valve. No matter how proficient the builder is in handling conflict, no matter how polished the builder's warranty systems and materials, it is always possible that someone just will not accept the builder's answer or proposed solution. One lawsuit will convince any builder that an alternative system for settling a disagreement is preferable to court.

A dispute resolution method can be specified in the warranty. When preparing such materials, builders should check applicable state laws that might affect details and wording of this section. Mediation is a less expensive method of dispute resolution than arbitration, but it also can be less binding. Somewhat less formal than a full court procedure, arbitration can save time, stress, and expense for both sides. It also usually engenders far less publicity than a court situation.

Insured warranties routinely carry a dispute-resolution clause. Local home builder association chapters sometimes offer dispute resolution services. Independent arbitration organizations offer yet another option, but builders should only consider those with experience in construction issues.

Learning from Conflict

Confrontations with customers are regrettable and should be prevented whenever possible. But they will occur. When they do, builders can take the opportunity to learn from them. Confrontation can be valuable if the builder takes time to dissect the conflict, trace it back to its causes, and analyze what happened.

Every customer conflict signifies two problems, both of which need to be addressed. First is the immediate conflict with this particular customer. Second is the possibility that some flaw in the builder's system (such as an employee who needs more training) may need adjustment to prevent a reoccurrence.

Occasional conflict is part of normal business. The famous 2 to 3 percent of people who cannot be satisfied really do seem to exist. Most of the time, however, builders can better manage their relationships with customers. By learning from conflicts, they can realize this objective.

Many potential conflicts can be avoided by organizing an effective warranty service program. As conflicts become fewer and farther between, and as the builder becomes better at handling them, a great deal of satisfaction will come from taking an angry customer through the process and turning that customer once again into a fan of the company. Effective conflict resolution can be used to reestablish a healthy relationship with each customer, maintain a good reputation, and increase repeat and referral business.

WARRANTY AS A DIAGNOSTIC TOOL

Just as the warranty department inherits the home, the customer, and the customer's opinion, it also inherits repair expenses. These reveal themselves a bit at a time as customers discover flaws in the product. To hold the warranty office responsible for keeping customers satisfied and costs down without allowing input into design and construction technique is unrealistic and unfair. Many warranty managers have changed jobs, if not careers, when held responsible for things they had no authority to influence.

It is equally unrealistic to turn control of the company over to warranty. A frustrated salesperson attending a staff meeting once said, "Just because one window leaked, the warranty office now wants us to build all our houses with no windows." Houses without windows would be less likely to leak; however, they might not sell very well. The desire to eliminate recurring items, inconvenience for customers, and unwanted work and expense must be balanced against consideration for initial costs, schedules, design appeal, and marketability.

In the past, most builders tolerated the existence of their warranty departments because of the legal obligation to fulfill their warranties. Now builders recognize that a well-run warranty program makes a significant contribution to the company's long-term success.

Expanding the Role of Warranty

Using current participative management techniques, builders can tap the experience and knowledge of warranty personnel in

171

reviewing new floor plans and spec sheets before making final decisions. Identifying a potential problem with an item does not mean that item is automatically eliminated from the design. If the item remains, however, everyone is more conscious of the risk it brings. Often, discussion of the risks can suggest an alternative or a solution.

In one situation, a floor plan that particularly appealed to young families included cafe doors between the kitchen and home entry. While the doors added a charming element to the home, young children quickly incorporated them into a noisy, dangerous game, racing between the kitchen, entry, and living room. Many homeowners ultimately begged to have them removed and the casing repaired. When the same doors showed up on another plan, employees reviewing the plans listened to the warranty staff's explanation about the customer complaints and compromised by designating the doors an optional feature. The doors still were shown in the model, and sales counselors mentioned the concerns of previous buyers when reviewing the option list in writing a contract. Some buyers decided against the doors; others did not. But because the choice—and the responsibility—now belonged to the home buyers, warranty stopped receiving complaints.

The intricate architectural detailing on today's homes can translate into a foundation plan that bears little resemblance to an ordinary rectangle. Each extra corner adds expense and a potential weak spot. Often, the same appearance can be achieved by cantilevering the subfloor over a simpler foundation. At the other extreme, long uninterrupted stretches of basement wall are vulnerable to damage from lateral soil pressure. While designers and architects may not have these factors uppermost in their minds, the warranty manager who approves the bills for engineer inspections and epoxy injection repairs is unlikely to overlook them.

A detailed agenda for working new subcontractors into the builder's system was outlined in chapter 6. The warranty department's participation in this process can be thought of as an investment in preventive care for the builder's reputation. No matter how quickly and effectively a builder responds when a sub disappoints a customer, that customer's goodwill is at risk. If the disappointment can be avoided, the risk is eliminated as well.

In addition to being available for technical answers to customer questions, the warranty office should provide the sales staff with regular updates on any changes in warranty policy, procedures, or standards. If the sales staff is to educate the customer, they must be kept informed about what that education should include.

Warranty's Role in Quality Control

As the contribution of the warranty function expands, one of the least glamorous, often most tedious, but potentially most beneficial aspects of this new role is in providing feedback about the performance of the product. Linking warranty personnel with those in design, purchasing, and construction closes the communication loop and allows the company to look at the results that accrue as homeowners live with its products.

Viewed as the last step in a comprehensive commitment to improving quality, warranty activities should include providing regular feedback about

- completion of walk-through items;
- recurring warranty claims related to a design element, a product, or any material used in construction; and
- subcontractors, in terms of both work quality and attitude toward homeowners.

An additional feedback opportunity often is overlooked. The warranty office can identify additional information or training that a sales staff may need to help them more accurately present the product. Sometimes a customer complains not because the home was not built as instructed, but because that customer had unclear or inaccurate perceptions of the builder's intentions and obligations. Warranty staff can provide insight that helps sales personnel refine or enhance their presentations to clarify such trouble spots.

Changing to Improve

To be truly helpful, a warranty department's report of a problem must be accompanied with suggestions for a solution. Objectivity and cooperation are keys to progress in the effort to improve product. Hunches, impressions, and assumptions have a place in this effort, but it is a small one. Similarly, a warranty manager's simply expressing frustration about having to fix the same problem over and over (and receiving complaints from the homeowners over and over) will be relatively useless when trying to convince construction, sales, or purchasing staff to make a change. A scientific approach produces faster and more satisfying results. Depending on the specific problem to be resolved, the warranty staff might take any or all of the following steps:

- State the specific problem.
- Identify the cause or causes, if known.
- Determine the cost to correct the problem, in terms of dollars and inconvenience to the customer. (For example, can the repair be completed in one visit, or will it require three? Does the problem endanger the homeowner or the homeowner's belongings? Is normal use of the home completely interrupted or just slightly inconvenienced? Does the problem lead to general condemnation of the company's competence or is it just another warranty headache?)
- Determine the frequency or number of times this problem has occurred.
- Identify potential solutions.
- Analyze each suggested solution as to cost, advantages, and disadvantages.
- Obtain comments from subs about scheduling implications and the availability of proposed materials.
- Consider additional relevant information, such as how other builders may be handling the same or a similar problem.

The warranty manager should summarize this information in as brief and succinct a memo as possible. Only the highlights are needed at this point. The memo should include a suggested meeting date and time to discuss the situation. The memo should be distributed to all staff members who have the authority to influence or make decisions that can resolve the issue. Typically, such a problem-solving memo and meeting would include a management-level person from construction, sales, and perhaps purchasing.

It is possible that a complete management review of the facts and options will lead to the conclusion that no change should be made. For example, this might be the conclusion if solving the problem would cost a lot of money per house and the problem represents only a minor inconvenience to a small percentage of the homeowners.

Should management choose to make a change in policy or procedure, the change must be implemented carefully. All affected parties must be made aware of what will change and why. If the change will be a major one, involving numerous procedures or employees, advance notification becomes even more important. Allowing employees to voice concerns and prepare for a major transition helps the change be accomplished more smoothly.

Simple inertia can obstruct many needed improvements. Thoroughly researching the necessary background information often can remove this obstacle. For example, one builder of traditional homes prided himself on using garage doors made of natural wood. This detail was assumed to be one of the points of quality that attracted buyers. The warranty department logged many hours spent sanding, priming and touching up paint as these doors began to show the effects of the harsh local climate. Cost information had no affect on the stagnant mentality, "We've always done it this way; our buyers expect it . . . ." Looking for a more convincing argument, the warranty department surveyed fifty homeowners and found that thirty-seven of them would have preferred a metal door for long-term ease of maintenance. Four additional homeowners did not even realize their garage doors were made of wood and indicated that they had no opinion either way. Purchasing documented a twenty-dollar cost savings with metal doors equal in appearance to the wood doors. Armed with this new, objective information, the warranty manager obtained approval and construction made the change.

Once a change is approved, the next step is to fully implement it. Solving an old problem by causing a new one will not result in progress. Two questions that help builders avoid such pitfalls are, "Who needs to know about this change?" and "What else must be done to carry this all the way through the system?"

In answering these questions the builder should check all possibilities, beginning with staff: purchasers, salespeople, accountants, draftspeople, decorators, subcontractors, and superintendents. Information available in model homes and all documents also should be checked, including the contract, homeowner manual, sales brochures, blueprints, and spec sheets for subs. Once all the related details have been identified, the builder can schedule the needed adjustments and work through the plan. The last step is to double-check all affected persons and procedures to confirm that the company has finished making the change.

Finally, the builder must not forget to consider whether any home buyers under contract will be surprised as a result of the change. Advising customers of a change and explaining the reasons behind it before they discover it at the walk-through will prevent conflict. Often, the buyer will happily accept the change. If the buyer has an objection, however, it is better to resolve the issue prior to the closing.

The insight that the warranty department can offer is too valuable for builders to ignore. Listening to feedback from warranty can spiral the company to improved products, greater customer satisfaction, and lower costs. This is the practical result of having a warranty department that strives to reduce the number and complexity of future warranty claims.

Pulling the Pieces Together

How often people say to themselves, "If I knew then what I know now . . . !" Many builders have learned the hard way that it can be embarrassing and expensive to overlook service performance. Waiting to realize this subject needs attention until homeowners are picketing the models is both painful and unnecessary. By assessing current warranty service performance, setting goals for improvement, and planning methods to meet those goals, such unpleasantness usually can be avoided.

The questions that follow may not all apply to all companies; builders and remodelers should simply skip those that are irrelevant to their situation. The questions and exercises that follow will reveal areas where a potential strength has gone undeveloped. In going through all of the questions, the first step is to clearly mark each one that applies. After the review has been completed, the builder can establish priorities for improving the service program.

Developing or Modifying the Organizational Chart

Where does warranty now fit with respect to the rest of the company? Does the department operate as part of the construction department or does it stand alone, neutral and independent? Diagram current lines of authority and check this aspect of organizational planning for balance. Is there a better way to organize?

> **Head Decision Maker:**

Warranty Personnel

List the members of the current warranty staff, and rate them in each of the categories shown. (Builders should develop their own rating scale based on norms established for their companies. Note: This tool is not intended for use in rating employee performance for purposes of hiring or compensation, and should never be used for such purposes. It is designed simply as a planning and management tool to identify areas of strength and weakness so that the builder can assess needs for further development or training.)

Employee	Attitude	Technical Knowledge	Administr. Procedures	Overall Productivity
(Manager)				
(Secretary)				
Technician(s):				

Answer the following questions:

1. With the exception of short seasonal peaks, are warranty personnel able to keep up with the workload within the desired time frame without working an excessive amount of overtime (evenings, weekends, holidays)? _____
2. Do service staff members have all necessary supplies and materials either on hand or readily available? _____
3. Are service technicians encouraged to ask questions of subcontractors, construction personnel, and others? Do they know whom to contact should something unusual arise? _____
4. Are comments from service personnel invited in management meetings? _____
5. Is training adequate? _____
6. What ongoing training or development activities are planned for the coming year?

_____

7. Are the personalities of warranty service employees appropriate for dealing with customers and handling continual questions, details, and occasional conflicts?

_____

8. Do warranty employees have sufficient authority over subs and adequate influence on the company's sales and construction efforts? (Is the warranty department's authority equal to its responsibility?) _____

9. To what extent are staff members empowered to make decisions and solve problems when those decisions involve expenses? (Note: Some companies set a preauthorized dollar amount that can be spent at the employee's discretion; others allow individual judgment, regardless of cost involved; still other permit no leeway at all.)

_____

10. Do customers override the warranty department's authority in order to get decisions reversed? _____
11. How frequently does this occur? _____
12. How often does this occur because an error was made in the first decision? _____
13. How often does this occur for other reasons?

_____

_____

Type of Warranty Coverage

1. Is the company's warranty self-insured or insured by an outside company? _____
2. How many homes are presently under each phase of warranty?
   _____ One-year materials and workmanship
   _____ Two-year mechanical
   _____ Structural
3. What kinds of coverage might the company be held liable for under implied warranty rulings or legislation?

_____

_____

Warranty Exposure

Calculate the total number of months of warranty obligation for all homes in the company's service program. Be sure to include a thirty-day grace period for each home. The chart below can be a helpful tool in figuring out this number. The extent of warranty exposure and its fluctuation can be significant for budgeting decisions and to project seasonal staff fluctuations.

To compute a company's warranty exposure, use the space in the top of the chart to write in the names of the upcoming 12 months (beginning with next month). Down the left side, list the communities where the company has homes under warranty. In the intersecting squares, tally every home that is under warranty. To allow for the grace period, remember to include each home in the tally for the box under the month *after* the warranty's home will expire.

For example, if a warranty expires in June, it would be included in the tally under under the July column. If a warranty expires this month, it would be marked in the first column—showing that the builder has one more month of obligation to that home. To record a home closing today, include it in the tally under the last column, indicating 13 months of exposure. (The "total" column at the far right serves as a check and balance
to be certain none of the homes in a given community has been left out.)

When all homes have been recorded, count the tally marks in each column. Multiply by the number shown on the bottom line. Finally, total the numbers across the bottom line. The sum is the warranty exposure, as measured in months.

Homes (by Month)

Community													Total
Total Homes:													

$\times$ months $\quad \times 1 \quad \times 2 \quad \times 3 \quad \times 4 \quad \times 5 \quad \times 6 \quad \times 7 \quad \times 8 \quad \times 9 \quad \times 10 \quad \times 11 \quad \times 12 \quad \times 13$

__ + __ + __ + __ + __ + __ + __ + __ + __ + __ + __ + __ + __ + __ =

Homeowner Warranty Information Resources

Having accurate information readily at hand makes service work proceed more smoothly and without delays or mistakes. Place a checkmark by each of the following information sources to which the company's warranty staff has ready access:

____ Individual warranty files
____ Contract/color selection sheet/options/change orders
____ Quality control inspections
____ Walk-through list
____ Warranty requests/letters
____ Phone logs or file reports
____ Correspondence to and from the customer
____ Inspection reports, photos/diagrams
____ Control sheets listing all homeowner addresses, telephone numbers, closing dates, and floor plan for quick reference
____ Purchasing manager for product/subcontractor specs
____ Construction personnel
____ Sales staff for information on contracts, change orders
____ Subcontractors
____ Manufacturer representatives
____ Building department inspectors
____ Building code manual
____ Engineer (soil, structural, or both)
____ Health department contact
____ County extension service contact
____ Company attorney

Support Systems

The people and items listed below are important parts of the infrastructure that supports effective warranty service. Rate the effectiveness of each in the company.

People and Departments

____ Receptionist
    ____ Answers promptly
    ____ Understands company procedures and does not comment on validity of homeowners' requests
    ____ Quickly channels calls to correct individual or office (adequately trained, provided up-to-date contact lists)
    ____ Takes accurate, complete messages
____ Secretary (Secretaries)
    ____ Correspondence, memos, and reports typed or processed quickly and accurately, attractively formatted for clear and effective presentation
    ____ Correct grammar, no typographical errors
    ____ Can identify and respond to priorities logically

_____ Communicates effectively across departmental lines
_____ Anticipates needed materials to prepare for routine reports and meetings
_____ Accounting
_____ Promptly pays approved invoices
_____ Processes back charges as directed
_____ Holds payments when directed to do so
_____ Issues authorized purchase orders or company checks when needed
_____ Prepares warranty budget for regular (at least quarterly) review

Printed Materials

_____ Customer Service Operations Manual
_____ Procedure in place for continuous revision
_____ Company customer philosophy (vision statement) included
_____ Objectives for each function in company identified
_____ Procedures simply and clearly outlined
_____ All necessary forms explained and samples included in logical order
_____ Job descriptions with clear, succinct definitions of responsibilities
_____ Used by staff on a regular basis
_____ Provided to all new staff
_____ Homeowner's Manual or Warranty Standards Introduction Packet
_____ Positive introduction
_____ Explanation of homeowner maintenance responsibilities
_____ Explanation of construction standards and builder responsibilities
_____ Other helpful items as noted (see Figure 4-10 for suggestions):

_____

_____

_____ Subcontractor Contract
_____ Warranty obligation(s) defined, including start date
_____ Critical subs obligated to 24-hour, seven-day coverage
_____ Specific number of business or calendar days assigned as time frame for completion of service orders
_____ Builder's recourse (steps for enforcement of contract) should work be completed in untimely or unsatisfactory manner
_____ Service standards and procedures (possibly in a separate memo that supplements the contract)

Procedures

Handling customer complaints involves receipt of the incoming report, analysis of the item(s) reported, response to the customer, and follow-up. Assess the company's processing procedures for each step, paying particular attention to timing. Prompt response is critically important to a good service image.

Incoming Reports

1. How do customers communicate with the company after move in regarding routine warranty items?

   _____

   _____

2. How do customers communicate with the company after move in regarding emergency items?

   _____

   _____

3. What structure has been developed to support routine warranty contact with homeowners?

   _____

   _____

4. How many phone calls does the warranty office receive each week?_____
5. What is the primary nature of those calls?

   _____

   _____

6. Do incoming telephone calls dominate staff time to the point that other tasks are neglected or unduly delayed?

   _____

   _____

7. In an average month how many letters or service requests are received?

   _____

   _____

8. List other contacts (For example, do customers drop off service requests at the sales or construction office?)

   _____

   _____

Analysis

1. By whom are warranty action decisions made? (List all that apply: The builder, warranty manager, service technicians)

   _____

   _____

2. Warranty action decisions generally are based on (check all that might apply):
   _____ Inspection   _____ Blueprints
   _____ Warranty standards   _____ Subs
   _____ Homeowner's Manual   _____ Construction
   _____ Tradition   _____ Sales
   _____ Contract   _____ Building codes
   _____ Manufacturer's Rep   _____ Other_____
3. Are builder-established policies adhered to in a reasonable manner?

   _____

   _____

4. How are difficult (judgment-call) or disputed warranty decisions resolved
   internally?

   _____

   _____

5. To what extent do personnel and departments other than warranty contribute to
   making warranty decisions?

   _____

   _____

6. Are company decisions ever based on "who" is asking for the service rather than
   on objective assessment of the facts and physical conditions?

   _____

   _____

7. Are warranty decisions ever based on how much the requested repair work will
   cost rather than an objective assessment of the facts and physical conditions?

   _____

   _____

Response

1. Are service orders written?_____
2. Calculate the average number of days from receipt of a routine request until
   _____ Inspection appointment made (if required)
   _____ Service order(s) issued (from original letter or inspection)
   _____ Denial letter sent (if appropriate)
   _____ Repair work completed
   _____ Reply given to information-only request
   _____ Follow-up call made or postcard sent to confirm satisfaction
   _____ Final documentation filed

3. Access to homes generally is available
   _____ by appointment only
   _____ using a key provided by the homeowner
   _____ combination (varies on homeowner, community, etc.)
4. List hours personnel are available for
   _____ inspections:
   _____ repairs:
5. What percentage of service work is completed by subcontractors? _____
6. Note the average response time for individual subs:
   HVAC   _____
   Plumber   _____
   Electrician   _____
   Drywall   _____
   Painter   _____
   Hardware   _____
   Cabinet   _____
   Floor Coverings   _____
   Windows and Screens   _____
   Roof and Gutter   _____
   Concrete   _____
   Other: _____   _____
7. Note the average response time for ALL subs: _____

Follow-up

1. What overall methods does the company use to make sure work is completed in a satisfactory fashion according to stated standards?

   _____

   _____

2. Specifically, who receives the report that the sub has completed the work?

   _____

3. Is this report given by telephone or in writing?

   _____

4. What steps are taken to enforce required deadlines and work quality standards?

   _____

   _____

5. Who obtains confirmation from the customer that the work is satisfactory, and how is the confirmation obtained?

   _____

   _____

6. What methods are used to identify recurring problems?

_____

_____

7. Is a particular employee responsible for analyzing options to eliminate recurring items?

_____

8. What opportunities do warranty employees have to suggest solutions that may affect other builder employees?

_____

_____

9. What is the response time from identification of a recurring problem to development of a solution?

_____

10. Is a regular (weekly or monthly) report prepared on service completions? _____ If so, to whom is it circulated?

_____

11. Does regular review of service completions affect hiring and retention of subs?

_____

Warranty Service Flow Chart

Develop a chart with entries that briefly describe each step in the company's current processing of routine warranty service requests (see Figure 6-8). Consider how each procedure might be improved to streamline processing or increase efficiency in other ways. After procedures needing improvement have been identified, consider the order in which changes should be implemented. (Developing a second chart showing how emergency situations are handled also can be useful.)

Procedures

Input:

_____

_____

Analysis:

_____

_____

Response:

_____

_____

_____

Follow-through:

_____

_____

_____

Master Service Calendar

The master service calendar (see Figure 6-7) is a one-page overview of warranty service activities that are performed on a regular, predictable basis. Create a calendar based on the model below and note what activities are completed daily, weekly, monthly, and annually. Could any of these activities be better handled if assigned within a different time frame? Are any activities omitted because of lack of staff?

DAILY	WEEKLY	MONTHLY	QUARTERLY	ANNUALLY

As a supplement to this chart, collect one copy of each form used in connection with warranty. Assemble them chronologically in a three-ring binder or other permanent storage format. Review them from the beginning. Which forms look out of place? Which forms have been updated recently and which are old? Can any two forms be combined to limit the paper work that must be handled? Are gaps apparent where a form or forms are needed?

One way to examine how closely the company complies with customer expectations is to determine how many requests are fulfilled.

1. Using a time frame of at least three but not more than six months, record
   - the average number of customer warranty requests each month   _____
   - the total number of items (not letters or telephone calls) for which service was requested   _____
   - the number or percentage of requests approved for warranty action   _____
   - the number or percentage of requests denied for warranty action   _____
2. Divide the number of items *approved* by the total number of items *requested* to find your position on the following customer service scale:

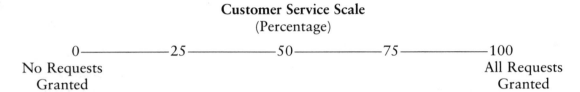

Customer Service Scale
(Percentage)

0————————25————————50————————75————————100
No Requests   All Requests
Granted   Granted

Few builders are found at either extreme of this customer service scale. At the 0 percent end is the builder who never gives the customer anything without a battle. At the 100 percent end is the builder who willingly gives customers anything they request. Operating at either extreme is dangerous for a business. Moreover, a healthy business will move up and down the scale (within a modest range) rather than remain static.

A low score may indicate that the warranty manager is too strict, or that the sales and warranty departments' educational efforts are not working. It is likely that customers are requesting inappropriate repairs they should already know will not be approved. To improve an extremely low score, step up efforts to alert customers to their home maintenance responsibilities and limits on warranty coverage before conflicts arise.

A very high score may indicate that personnel have become intimidated by customers' aggressive tactics—or that overloaded staff are granting requests without fully examining their validity. When trying to tighten policies on approval of warranty requests, some time spent training employees can help ensure that new policies are applied consistently and effectively, with the support of the whole organization.

A company's position on the scale reflects the interaction of customers' expectations with the builder's warranty policy and philosophy. The builder determines the answers, but the customers determine the questions. By thoroughly and fairly educating customers, thereby adjusting their expectations prior to entering into the contract, builders can greatly influence their customers' warranty requests.

By educating the customer, builders position themselves favorably in the marketplace. The builder is perceived as saying "yes" more often; actually, the customer has been educated to make fewer inappropriate requests.

Builder Service Goals

To identify service goals, review the notes made in this assessment of the company's current service performance. Under each heading, determine if a change would improve service quality or efficiency. List the changes to be considered. (On the form that follows, space is provided for up to three changes under each heading. (Builders will find that some areas require fewer improvements—perhaps none—while other areas may require more.) How will each proposed change affect the warranty function?

Changes to Consider

Organizational Chart

1. _____
2. _____
3. _____

Warranty Personnel

1. _____
2. _____
3. _____

Homeowner Warranty Information Resources

1. _____
2. _____
3. _____

Support Systems

   People and Departments

   1. _____
   2. _____
   3. _____

   Printed Materials

   1. _____
   2. _____
   3. _____

Procedures

   Input

   1. _____
   2. _____

3. _____

Analysis

1. _____

2. _____

3. _____

Response

1. _____

2. _____

3. _____

Follow-through

1. _____

2. _____

3. _____

Master Service Calendar

1. _____

2. _____

3. _____

Once all the goals are identified, rank them. It is impossible to work on everything at once. Also, it is impractical to think that a system currently delivering service in 102 days can be changed overnight to a system that delivers service in 21 days.

When the goals have been put in order of importance, the next step is to list the tasks that must be accomplished to reach each goal. Then, identifying obstacles to each task, the builder can analyze how best to eliminate or overcome those obstacles. A carefully thought-out strategy can result in quick progress.

Check to be sure that the materials or equipment and staff needed to accomplish the goals are available. If materials are missing, acquire them; if staff are needed, assign or hire them. In modifying or developing new materials, always be sure to obtain comments from the people who will be using them.

Create a tentative schedule for achieving each step toward the desired goals. In implementing any change, it is important to monitor progress toward the goal; to manage that process, the builder can delegate responsibilities. Establish who on staff will oversee each improvement, and at what intervals the person should provide updates. If delays occur, the builder should analyze their causes to identify and remove any remaining obstacles to change. The worksheet that follows helps organize the information from goal-setting through updates into a format convenient for tracking.

Builder Service Goal Worksheet

Subject:

_____

_____

_____

Goal:

_____

_____

_____

Strategy:

_____

_____

_____

Items Needed:

_____

_____

_____

Proposed Schedule:

_____

_____

_____

Progress:

- Staff Person Responsible:_____
- Scheduled Updates:_____
- Update 1:_____
- Update 2:_____
- Update 3:_____
- Update 4:_____

Notes:

_____

_____

_____